Books *Plus*

100 Extension Activities in Art, Drama, Music, Math, and Science

SUE McCLEAF NESPECA

JOAN B. REEVE

AMERICAN LIBRARY ASSOCIATION
Chicago   2003

Design and composition by ALA Editions in ITC Legacy Sans and Helvetica Condensed using QuarkXPress 4.1 for the PC

Illustrations by Richard Laurent

Printed on 50-pound white offset, a pH-neutral stock, and 10-point cover stock by McNaughton & Gunn

The paper used in this publication meets the minimum requirements of American National Standard for Information Sciences—Permanence of Paper for Printed Library Materials, ANSI Z39.48-1992. ∞

Library of Congress Cataloging-in-Publication Data

Nespeca, Sue McCleaf.
    Picture books plus : 100 extension activities in art, drama, music, math, and science / Sue McCleaf Nespeca, Joan B. Reeve.
        p.   cm.
    Includes bibliographical references and index.
    ISBN 0-8389-0840-3
    1. Picture books for children—Educational aspects. 2. Education, Elementary—Activity programs. 3. School children—Books and reading.   I. Reeve, Joan B. II. Title.
    LB1044.9.P49 N47 2003
    372.13—dc21   2002011822

07   06   05   04   03   5   4   3   2   1

To Mom
(also known as Aunt Elizabeth to Joan),
Dad
(also known as Uncle Crowell to Sue),
and of course to
Gil, Rebo, Ben, and Adam

Contents

Figures

Acknowledgments

Thanks go to staff members of Adams County Public Library, Gettysburg, Pennsylvania, particularly Nancy Newman, for assistance in obtaining copies of some of the picture books listed. Though we own most of the books mentioned in this work, library staff were always friendly and willing to secure copies of the few titles we do not have. Also, we would like to acknowledge several staff members of the Gettysburg Area School District—Harriett Cameron, Sue Yingling, Heather Tschop, and Patti Myers—for their help in relaying messages and answering questions including computer difficulties. Thanks to the staff at NOLA Regional Library System, Warren, Ohio, for their support, particularly Paul Pormen, Director, for his assistance with digital photography of some of the art for illustrations, and Elaine Casterline for her help in answering questions about musical CDs and cassettes for titles we knew but could not remember. Also, we wish to express our appreciation to Pastor Clifton Eschbach for his support and guidance. To our editor Karen Young, we appreciate the advice and suggestions given to us. Finally, thanks to Mom (Aunt Elizabeth) for the use of her kitchen and supplies for testing experiments and trying out our activities and for the many, many weeks we were camped out on her dining room table with numerous crates of books filling her living room and sunporch.

Introduction

We have been avid fans of sharing picture books with children for over twenty-five years. For at least a dozen years, we have seen the wisdom of using extensions with picture books. Extensions allow children to think about a book in a new way. They extend and reinforce the content of the story and aid in comprehension. Extensions provide a natural tie-in to various areas of the curriculum. Most importantly, extensions motivate children to read and, thus, promote the love and joy of sharing books.

Think of a popular children's television show, such as *Arthur,* on the public broadcasting network. Not only does the television show (an extension of the books by that name) increase readership of the many books in that series, but related merchandising (again, forms of extensions) also cause children to check out Arthur books by the handful. Thus, all these forms of extensions motivate children to read (or listen to) more literature.

CHAPTER STRUCTURE

Picture Books Plus focuses on five curricula—art, drama, music, math, and science, because we feel these areas will appeal most to public and school librarians, to teachers and early childhood educators, and, of course, to children, with their natural curiosity and energy. Each chapter includes twenty picture book titles along with a short annotation of the book, an extension in at least one of the five subject areas, any materials needed, and the procedure to conduct the extension. Every activity in this book was tested (some several times). This allowed us to give hints on how to better execute the activity in a section titled "Recommendations." An additional extension that could also be carried out follows. Readers may want to do just the additional extension

and not the original one suggested. For example, in the math chapter, we recommend a book titled *Five Creatures,* which describes the various members of a household and their similar and dissimilar characteristics and traits. This is followed by an activity involving a Venn diagram. The additional extension involves children sharing information about the family members who share their households along with an activity related to making a family tree and the suggestion to sing the song "Family Tree," by Tom Chapin. In a public library setting, the storyteller may share the title and then just share the song "Family Tree" rather than involving children with the Venn diagram. By having several different activities for each featured picture book, most readers will find at least one activity they will want to do with each recommended title.

At the end of each chapter is a list of every picture book that was used either in the extension or recommended in an additional extension. From chapter 2 on, each chapter also includes a list of the musical recordings or videos used in the extensions. Finally, each chapter closes with a list of resource books that will lead readers to further activities or ways to best convey a certain subject area to young children. We encourage you to examine some of these resource books for more activities.

SELECTION CRITERIA

We very carefully chose the 100 picture books (20 titles for each subject area) based on the quality of their writing and the excellence of their illustrations and their appeal to a broad age range of children. We also wanted to include diversity and avoid stereotyping. Of course, you should preview the book first, practice it several times, and then share the story with the children before doing the extension activity. Although we carefully checked the in-print status of every picture book and resource book recommended, books can go out of print very quickly. Therefore, some of the recommended picture books may be out of print before this book is. However, because we picked quality titles that are well duplicated, you should be able to secure most of the titles recommended, even if some have gone out of print.

AUDIENCE

Picture Books Plus is directed to those teachers, librarians, or adults who live or work with children preschool age through grade three. These ages were selected because picture books have the most appeal to young children, defined by the National Association for the Education of Young Children as children preschool age through grade three. However, quality picture books should be used with all ages—from the very young through adult ages—not only because of the text, but also because they are beautiful works of art. In fact, both the authors' favorite books to read are picture books. Therefore, the recommended books and extensions can be used with children older than third grade. In fact, some of the activities have definite potential for much older children. However, when the text recommends an activity as being "best for younger children," it means the younger of the ages targeted (preschool through approximately grade one). If the activity is recommended for older children, we are referring to the upper grades of the intended range (grades two, three, and above).

This book will be of use to anyone interested in children's literature and anyone who feels it is important for children to have many literacy experiences. The primary focus is for public librarians; school media specialists; teachers of young children in public schools, preschools, Head Start centers, day-care or home-care settings, or home-schooling situations; and parents. It is also of value for teachers and students in education and library science programs, students in child development programs, and academic libraries that support education and library science programs.

Following are some suggestions of ways to use this book in two specific settings—public libraries and schools.

Picture Books Plus and Public Libraries

Public libraries across the country are recognizing the importance of making programs more developmentally appropriate for children by using techniques incorporated by early childhood educators and having more opportunities for hands-on learning experiences. Many librarians are now incorporating art, math, or science activities after sharing literature with children. This book will help librarians learn about the types of books to share and the types of activities that make good extensions. (This is not something typically taught in library school, and not all librarians have an early childhood background.)

Several national initiatives in the past few years have emphasized the literature/curriculum theme. For example, the Vermont Center for the Book has established such programs as "Ask Mother Goose Why?" (a science-literature program) and "You Can Count on Mother Goose" (a math-literature program). Also, the American Library Association's (ALA) Office of Public Programs and its Association for Library Service to Children recently cooperated with the Minnesota Children's Museum on a children's museum and public library exhibit titled "Go Figure!" (a math-literature exhibit). This was ALA's first traveling exhibit geared toward young children, their parents, and caregivers. Librarians who have seen these national programs are attempting to incorporate more subject-based programming in their libraries.

Here are some ways you could use *Picture Books Plus* in public library programming:

> Share one extension after reading one of the titles in a normal story-time program.
>
> Plan an entire story-time program based on books with extensions.
>
> Plan an entire program based on a subject area, and share books and activities from that subject area (e.g., Science Fun Night).
>
> Use extensions in family story time or family programming, which is becoming more popular in libraries (these books and extensions are ideal for family programming).

Plan a program for early childhood educators by sharing books and extensions.

Plan a program for college students majoring in early childhood or elementary education.

Present a program to homeschoolers.

Present a program to parents (e.g., offer ideas for open-ended art projects and books).

Present a program to schoolteachers on using picture books across the curriculum.

Present a program to graduate students in library science.

Picture Books Plus and Schools

In U.S. schools, much emphasis is placed on incorporating literature across the curriculum. There never seems to be enough time in a teacher's day to cover every element of the curriculum to the depth and breadth that is often needed to reach the needs of each student. For this reason, curriculum compaction has become a suggested remedy. To accomplish this, teachers need help from their school media specialists with ideas on the best books to choose. Suggesting extensions as follow-up activities for the books will be a welcome extra.

A demand exists for books that integrate literature with math and science. Moreover, children thrive best when art, drama, and music are a planned part of their day. Using the ideas in *Picture Books Plus* allows for optimum experiences in each of these areas.

Here are some suggestions on how to use this book in school settings:

School librarians could share a story and extension with pupils during a library period.

School librarians could present a program to teachers on good books to use across the curriculum.

School librarians could present a literature-based program and perform some of the extensions for teachers.

Curriculum specialists could consult this book for potential in-service presentations.

A literature-extension program could be presented to Parent-Teacher Associations.

Teachers could use this book to make a list of reading suggestions for their classes based on their curricular needs.

Teachers could use this book to make a list of reading suggestions for parents.

Teachers could use this book to enhance lesson plans.

Teachers could use this book as a ready source for songs, recipes, a few simple dance steps (in addition to many other literacy activities), *and* some great books.

These are just a few ways this book will be useful for both public libraries and schools. You will find other uses, and we would welcome hearing your ideas (contact us at sue@kidlitplus.com and jebo@supernet.com).

We hope this book motivates you to increase your use of children's literature. We firmly believe in the importance of immersing children in quality literature and in extending these books to increase children's literacy experiences. While performing these hands-on activities, you will be presenting children with vocabulary they will see in print later when they become independent readers. Also, when sharing picture books, children are exposed to incredible art, different media, and diverse art techniques. These extensions allow for numerous "teachable moments." Have fun with these books and activities!

Chapter One

~ ✑ ~ ✑ ~

Why Use Picture
Books with Children?

One of the best ways to interest young children in reading picture books is to read picture books to them. By exposing children to a wealth of quality literature, the chances improve that they will become readers themselves. To have children enjoy literature is a worthwhile goal, but if you actually *engage* them in literature in a way they find pleasurable, the chances are greater still that they will desire to become avid readers. That is why it is important to both read picture books and extend the books with activities that combine learning and fun. The activities in the following chapters allow for many and varied literacy experiences.

Before children learn to read text, they "read" the illustrations in picture books. Thus, one of children's first steps in learning to read text is to read pictures. It is important to provide these experiences to children from birth on. As they get older and are exposed to more books, they begin to notice print and discover that print carries meaning. They gain the opportunity to hear and read about people, places, and cultures that are both similar to and different from their own. Exposing them to picture books increases their view of the world, creating those important neural pathways in the brain that are essential to raise

intelligence levels and can only be enhanced during the window of opportunity available to the young child.

BENEFITS OF SHARING PICTURE BOOKS WITH CHILDREN

In addition to the sheer pleasure of sharing a book with others, children benefit in a variety of ways from the exposure to picture books. The following are some of the benefits of sharing high-quality picture books with children.

It increases their language development.

Children are exposed to excellent works of art through the illustrations.

Children are exposed to a variety of interesting writing styles.

They learn about the structure and form of literature.

They are introduced to literary elements such as plot, characterization, setting, theme, and style.

Children are introduced to literature, which increases their desire for independent reading.

Reading to children enhances their later reading achievement.

PICTURE BOOK DEFINITION

A picture book contains both text and illustrations that complement each other and work together as a whole unit. The illustrations are integral to the story and must match the text.

Two excellent definitions of picture books come from authorities who have written noted works on picture books:

A picture book is text, illustrations, total design; an item of manufacture and a commercial product; a social, cultural, historical document; and foremost an experience for a child. As an art form it hinges on the interdependence of pictures and words, on the simultaneous display of two facing pages, and on the drama of the turning page.[1]

The picture book is an unique art object, a combination of image and idea that allows the reader to come away with more than the sum of the parts. We can no more look at a single illustration in the book or examine the words without the pictures than we can view 5 minutes of a 2-hour film or see an opera without hearing the singers' voices and say we have experienced the whole. The picture book is unique, and our experience of it will be something magical and personal, one that will change with each reading.[2]

QUALITY IN PICTURE BOOKS

Important characteristics to look for when choosing quality picture books include the following:

They appeal to a wide age range.

The story is original or the well-done adaptation of a classic original.

The story has universal appeal.

The text and illustrations match and are integrated.

The illustrations are appropriate to the story and for the intended audience.

The illustrations are of high artistic quality.

There is a good use of visual elements.

The theme is of interest to children.

The subject matter is appropriate for children.

The story uses rich vocabulary.

The story is imaginative.

There is a good plot.

There is good characterization.

There is predictability to the text.

There is repetition, rhythm or rhyme, alliteration, or other devices children enjoy.

The binding is superior.

Illustrations are not lost in the gutter of the book.

The illustrations are large enough for children to see.

The book has good design qualities.

What are some other considerations when evaluating picture books? We would like to recommend two sources to consider when evaluating picture books and their illustrations: *Children's Literature in the Elementary School,* by Charlotte S. Huck et al., and Kathleen T. Horning's *From Cover to Cover.* (*See* "Resource Books on Children's Picture Books and Art" at the end of the chapter.)

HOW TO SHARE PICTURE BOOKS WITH CHILDREN

Here are tips to use when sharing picture books with children:

Hold the book so that all children can see the pictures.

Involve the children in the telling if possible (have them repeat a refrain or make a sound, etc.).

Make eye contact with the children.

Read with expression.

Use different voices for different characters.

Emphasize certain words for effect.

Clarify vocabulary as needed within the context of the story.

Keep questions and comments to a minimum during the story to allow children to follow the flow of the story.

Practice the story several times before sharing it so that you know the text well.

Be prepared to reread favorites.

PICTURE BOOK ART

The art in picture books is one of the most important reasons to share picture books with children. Many children do not have the opportunity to visit fine art galleries, and yet, with picture books, they are exposed to some of the finest art in the world. They can discover many different styles of art, even though they might not know the names of the various styles. From realism, impressionism, expressionism, abstract art, surrealism, primitive art, and folk art to cartoons, there are picture books to be found that depict all these different styles. Zena Sutherland, an authority on children's literature, states that "a wonderful way to teach art appreciation would be through children's picture books which run the whole gamut of styles and techniques."[3]

The art is an integral part of the picture book, and thus it is important to consider the quality of the illustrations when choosing picture books to share. Some of the elements that illustrators must consider in addition to style are visual elements, format, and type of medium (or mixed media) used.

Visual Elements

The artist uses visual elements to help tell the story. They include line, color, shape, texture, composition or design, space, value, and perspective.

Line—Lines can be thick or thin, short or long, light or dark, straight or curved, horizontal or vertical, flowing or jagged, and so forth.

Color or Hue—Though some illustrators work in gradations of black and white, most work with color. Color helps to establish mood, such as using warm colors (red, yellow, or orange) or cool colors (green, blue, or purple). Artists can make variations of colors by adding white (tint), black (shade), or gray (tone).

Shape—Shapes may be flat or two-dimensional, geometrical, irregular, or curving.

Texture—Artists can visually add texture to their work by making objects smooth or hard, rough or soft. Line, color, and shape can be manipulated, or the medium the artist uses may also give the effect of texture.

Composition or Design—This is the way the artist arranges the pictorial elements, assembling all the parts to make a whole, while using various design principles to create an effect.

Space—Illustrators make great use of space by choosing whether to create a feeling of depth, allowing the surface to appear three-dimensional or flat. They consider the effect of employing white versus dark spaces in creating the mood.

Value—Value is the amount of lightness or darkness the artist uses. It can also create a mood or add energy to a picture.

Perspective—An artist uses perspective to establish the painting's point of view, just as an author uses point of view to tell the story.

Format

When considering the art and design of a picture book, you need to consider the picture book as a whole because other properties of the book contribute to the final product.

Cover—Despite the saying, "You can't judge a book by its cover," the cover does entice the reader and gives the first impression of the book.

Endpapers—The endpapers are the pages directly inside the front and back cover and are fastened to the opposite sides of the cover. Some illustrators use the endpapers as part of the story. Librarians who buy picture books already prebound often lose the beauty of the endpapers when the front and back covers are cut off and the manufacturer's binding is added.

Page Layout—The way the text and illustrations are placed add to the flow of the story. Some illustrators use single-page spreads, others use double-page spreads, and some alternate between the two. Artists will sometimes employ borders around their works, and certain illustrators even tell a separate story or use them as a predictor of future events.

Typeface and Typography—The art or design editor will normally help to select a typeface or font to be used for the text. Recent picture books have had moving typeface (type that moves in swirls or circular patterns, varies in size, or meanders across the page) or fonts that changed size within the page, both of which are design elements that correlated with the story.

Size—The size of the book will often denote the age of the audience for whom the book is intended. Toddlers need small board books they can hold in their hands. Large picture books may be good for group sharing. The size may also have something to do with the theme of the book.

Book Shape—Some books actually employ a shape that corresponds to the story.

Page Shape—Different artists have used unique page shapes (half pages, accordion-style pages, pages with die-cut holes, etc.) for a visual effect that adds meaning to the text.

Type of Paper—The quality of the paper and the type of paper stock used can make a difference in the presentation of the text.

Texture—Several authors add raised areas for children to touch and feel.

Different Types of Media

Illustrators of children's picture books work in various different media or may use mixed media. Following are some of the more common types of illustrations and their media used today.

PAINTING

Oil—Powdered color mixed with oils and resins

Watercolor—Powdered color mixed with gum arabic and glycerine and then applied with water

Acrylics—Powdered color mixed with synthetic (vinyl) resin (sometimes diluted with water) and that dries much faster than oils

Tempera—Powdered color ground with water and mixed with egg yolk or egg white

Gouache—Powdered color made opaque with the addition of white (often chalk)

DRAWING

Pen and Ink—Often used to draw a picture that is subsequently painted

Pencils—May be made with graphite or carbon, or the artist may use colored pencils

Crayons—Made from pigment and paraffin wax

Charcoals—Traditionally made from charred twigs

Pastels—Powdered color mixed with white chalk and bound with gum

PRINTING

Woodcuts—A design is drawn in reverse on a wood surface, and then the rest of the wood surface that will not be printed is cut away. Raised surfaces are then inked and pressed on paper.

Linoleum Cuts—Identical to woodcuts, except a linoleum block is used

Scratchboard—Has two layers of board (black and white or black and multicolored). The artist uses a sharp instrument to scratch an illustration on the top layer, thus revealing portions of the bottom layer. Some artists use color washes over the illustration.

CLOTH

Fabric—Different types of fabric (usually with very different textures) are used to construct pictures.

Batik—Hot wax resist technique where designs are drawn on fabric with hot wax and then immersed in dye. The process is usually repeated several times with additional layers of wax. The crackling of the wax surface allows the dye to penetrate, creating surprising effects.

PHOTOGRAPHY

Black-and-white or color photography (catching scenes on film with light)

COLLAGE

Pieces of paper, fabric, or materials of various weights or textures are attached to a background.

SCULPTURE

Plasticine—Similar to clay but non-hardening

COMPUTER-GENERATED ART

A newer technique where the illustrator generates all the illustrations by using graphic software on a computer

For more information on artistic media used in picture books, consult <http://picturingbooks. imaginarylands.org/media/media.html>. Chapter 2, "Extending Picture Books through Art," recommends ways for children to explore some of these different types of media.

Notes

1. Barbara Bader, *American Picturebooks: From Noah's Ark to the Beast Within* (New York: Macmillan, 1976), 1.

2. Barbara Z. Kiefer, *The Potential of Picturebooks* (Englewood Cliffs, N.J.: Prentice-Hall, 1995), 6.

3. Zena Sutherland, *Children and Books* (Glenview, Ill.: Scott, Foresman, 1977), 2.

Resource Books on Children's Picture Books and Art

Horning, Kathleen T. *From Cover to Cover: Evaluating and Reviewing Children's Books.* New York: HarperCollins, 1997.

Huck, Charlotte S., Susan Hepler, Janet Hickman, and Barbara Z. Kiefer. *Children's Literature in the Elementary School.* 7th ed. Boston: McGraw-Hill, 2001.

Kiefer, Barbara Z. *The Potential of Picturebooks: From Visual Literacy to Aesthetic Understanding.* Englewood Cliffs, N.J.: Prentice-Hall, 1995.

Stewig, John Warren. *Looking at Picture Books.* Fort Atkinson, Wis.: Highsmith, 1995.

Resource Books for Art Techniques Used in Picture Books

Association for Library Service to Children. *The Newbery and Caldecott Awards: A Guide to the Medal and Honor Books.* Chicago: American Library Assn. Issued annually.

Cianciolo, Patricia. *Picture Books for Children.* 4th ed. Chicago: American Library Assn., 1997.

Cummins, Julie. *Children's Book Illustration and Design.* Oxnard, Calif.: PBC International, 1997.

Chapter Two

Extending Picture Books through Art

Young children's art is a wonderful, often messy, fun process! It involves use of motor skills and creativity as well as experimentation, and it leads to language development of words used for classification. Working with children in art also requires a few warnings about dangers, not only physical ones, but also dangers to a child's talents and interest in art.

Art is such a natural subject for integration of other curricula areas. It nurtures the relationship to math and spatial thinking. Art provides lessons in science concepts. It is often a social event. It can be used in planning and presenting both writing and drama. Art develops hand strength and coordination. It leads to good self-esteem also, because everyone *can* be an artist.

EMBRACING THE PROCESS OF CREATING ART

The most important thought to keep in mind when working with children in art is that their energies are involved in a *process* of movement and manipulation of materials that supersedes whatever appearance the finished *product* may take. The goal is to have the children feel satisfied about their creative expressions.

Joan reassures the parents of her kindergartners that she often sees the beautiful colors of her students' work turn to brown as they continue to add layers of paint colors. The product looks dull, but the process was full of color and design. The same holds true for work with dough; many glorious shapes are molded with care despite the "lumps" that may remain when the sculptures are finished.

When beginning an art project with new materials, the children should be given time to freely explore and test the new substance or procedure. Children's inexperience with the qualities and feel of materials and their abilities to apply and change them by their uses dictate that they have a chance to experiment with the materials on their own to discover the properties, without the expectation of anything else initially. This is a good time to discuss classification words to describe the color, shape, size, and texture. These are all words that the children will need in their personal language to describe what they encounter and will see in print as they read, now or later.

As children explore, they use important muscle skills to develop both hand-to-eye coordination and the pincer grip of thumb meeting forefinger that is so important in handwriting comfort and control. Visual motor skills develop as their hands attempt to reproduce what they see in their environment or translate something with their own creativity.

DEVELOPING AN ENVIRONMENT THAT NURTURES CREATIVITY

Speaking of creativity, we should note the long-lasting effects that adults' comments can have on children. Sue clearly remembers her art experiences from grade school. When she was unable to reproduce what the teacher expected in art, she came to the conclusion that she was not artistic and established a lifelong pattern of stating, "I am not artistic" or "I cannot draw." If Sue would have been free to explore materials and not meet teachers' models or expectations on how something should look, she might not have closed her mind to her artistic expressions.

Though there certainly is a place for art and craft projects in libraries, the emphasis seems to be on projects that require children to paste or glue precut items to other objects or to use coloring pages. When these are used, children have little chance for creativity. Outside of learning how to follow directions, children can feel little satisfaction in their creations, and every child's project looks the same if done "correctly"—just like the librarian model! Children tend to throw these away if they feel no ownership of the work. We highly encourage librarians and teachers to reconsider these projects and move toward "process-oriented projects" rather than "product-oriented models." Not only will the children have a wonderful opportunity to explore different art media, but they will also have more chances for creativity, and your library programs will be more developmentally appropriate. The results will be visually interesting, too, with each child's finished project looking unique instead of appearing like cookie-cutter art.

IMPORTANT DO'S AND DON'TS

The interactions between the teacher or librarian and the children can greatly enhance the children's experiences and attitudes. The following suggestions may be helpful as you interact with the children's results.

Do ask them to tell you about their work.

Do not ask, "What is *this* supposed to be?" or tell them it just looks like scribbles.

Do ask, "What do you like best about your work today?"

Do respect *their* work; for example, ask permission before adding their names or other writing to it.

Do not set up a competitive atmosphere by praising one child's art abilities. This can also put undue pressure on this child to perform for you rather than for his or her satisfaction or pleasure.

Do not emphasize making the work look like your model, if you choose to use one. We rarely do this, preferring to allow children to explore the medium for themselves. There is no right or wrong way in artistic expression.

Do show examples of fine art in your library or school. This shows children techniques that the masters have used successfully and allows visual enjoyment of beautiful works. Add vocabulary specific to the arts: collage, stencil, watercolor, woodcut, etching, scratchboard, and so forth. Viewing fine art can lead to a lifelong appreciation of art's effects on their surroundings, watching for colors and patterns in nature as well as the mood of decorations within their homes. Creating and displaying art will enrich both their careers and home lives. "The very young child does have the ability to create, view, interpret, and appreciate fine art. When these abilities are respected and fostered by the early childhood teacher, children will develop their abilities to observe, verbally express, and draw conclusions across all learning disciplines, as well as to embrace a lifelong love of art."[1]

Do notice things about their work, saying, for instance, "I see that you used blues and greens in your work. Those are two of the 'cool' colors. Do you see how you made them swirl in this part of your work?"

Do not tell them that you *like* their work, because you are not the person they should be seeking to please, but rather themselves. If they ask you if you like it, turn their questions around by asking how they feel about what they've accomplished.

Do be enthusiastic about the process: "Look at the *reds* you have used!"

Do let the children choose the surface (colors, sizes, or types of paper or other materials), medium (paint, crayons, pencils, or markers, etc.), and tools that they will use. In addition to the obvious boost for creativity, you are also providing valuable experiences in decision making. This may not seem so very important now, but think of the many decisions required of them as teenagers. Children need the practice now, when the choices are small and safe ones. It leads to their successful independence and increases their confidence in their ability to make good choices.

MATERIALS AND TOOLS

When choosing materials and tools, consider the ages of the children with whom you work. Make sure everything is age-appropriate. Follow the guidelines suggested on packaging. Of course, be careful with hot irons or glue guns and sharp edges on wood, metal, and other materials. Use safety scissors. Parents will be happier if you purchase washable paints and markers because they will get on the children's clothing (and bodies) sometimes, despite the use of smocks. We use donated shirts worn backward and fastened just at the neck, T-shirts that cover the child front and back, or large garbage bags with neck and arm holes cut out. (Be sure to supervise young children with plastic bags.) These can be stored in a box on a shelf where they are readily accessible to the children (and teach the children to return them there when they are through with them).

Recycling or adapting by using materials on hand keeps costs down, and teaches children about protecting resources. Look for versatile items that might normally be thrown away, but that children would find delightful. Resource books have lists of such materials. One source is *Good Earth Art,* by Mary Ann Kohl (*see* "Art Resource Books" at the end of the chapter).

ART TECHNIQUES AND COLOR

In our extensions, we use various art techniques and colors. The following list offers a brief description of a variety of techniques.

Collage—Pasting various materials and textures onto a picture's surface

Computer-Generated Art—Using tools found in drawing and painting programs to produce, change, reproduce, and color pictures

Cut Paper—Using specially, often intricately, cut layers of paper to build a picture

Drawing and Coloring—After choosing from various media (pencils, charcoal, colored pencils, crayons, markers, etc.), completing a line drawing and, if desired, adding hues, tints, and shadings

Finger Painting—Using all parts of the hands to spread various tactile liquids across paper to form designs

Iron-On Transfers—Turning a waxy crayon drawing facedown on an absorbent surface and applying heat to the back of the drawing to print the image onto the new surface

Mirror Images—Reproducing in reverse by placing a mirror's edge along an object or picture and viewing the result as a whole or using a computer drawing program to flip portions of the picture and align them beside their (reversed) doubles

Origami—Folding paper into specific shapes that mimic real-life objects

Painting—Using various materials for brushes, paints, and surfaces

Papermaking—Grinding recycled paper with water to form pulp; then draining, pressing, and drying into a "new" sheet of paper

Pop-Ups or Movables—Folding, cutting, attaching, and causing parts of the picture to stand out from the rest of the picture or to move with the use of a "handle"

Printmaking—Cutting away parts of a flat surface, inking the remaining surface, and pressing it onto another surface to make an image that may be repeated to form a pattern

Raised Relief—Adding various materials onto a surface to provide a texture that can be felt when touched

Rubbings—Laying paper over a textured surface and rubbing with the side of a crayon or a soft pencil to cause the design below to show through on the paper as darkened areas

Scratchboard Art—Scratching the black from the scratchboard with any awl-like instrument, allowing the white or colors below to show (used very effectively in Brian Pinkney's award-winning illustrations)

Three-Dimensional Art—Showing depth as well as height and width

Tracing Forms—Holding a stencil or an object steady with your nondominant hand as you draw a line completely around it using your dominant hand (a skill for young children to learn)

When creating art using any of the above techniques, remember to consider properties of color. Color can create a mood and help to tell a story, among other things. For help with choosing contrasting and complementary colors, keep an inexpensive color wheel on hand.

A basic color wheel contains these colors in a circle: red, orange, yellow, green, blue, and purple. Cool colors are one side of the wheel: greens, blues, and purples; warm colors are the other side: reds, oranges, and yellows. Primary colors—red, yellow, and blue—are those that can be used to mix the secondary colors: orange, green, and purple. If equal amounts of either primary or secondary colors are mixed, they will form brown. Complementary colors are those that are across from each other on the color wheel: red and green, orange and blue, yellow and purple. White and black may be added to any color to provide tints and shades. Grays and beige or tan are considered neutral colors.

CONSIDERATIONS FOR OUR ART EXTENSIONS

There are several different illustrated versions of some of the books presented in our art extensions. Please note this when you choose a book. For example, if you want to see the basis for the stained-glass effect that we model for *There Was an Old Lady Who Swallowed a Fly,* you *must* use the version listed that Simms Taback illustrated. On the other hand, if your favorite books are similar to the ones we have chosen, you may decide to use them instead or show them as another example of the process.

Just remember to avoid the trap of an emphasis on product over process—the objective is to have fun and learn something about art. Make sure the families understand this, too. Now, enjoy using our art extensions for the following twenty picture books!

ART EXTENSIONS

Alison's Zinnia
Anita Lobel (Greenwillow)
OR USE
Planting a Rainbow
Lois Ehlert (Harcourt Brace)

This entire book follows a clever alphabet pattern (girl-verb-flower). A child whose name begins with the letter A performs an action that is described with a verb beginning with the letter A; the child then gives the flower, whose name begins with the letter A, to a child whose name begins with the letter B.

EXTENSION: Coffee Filter Flowers

MATERIALS

> large coffee filters
> rubbing alcohol
> food colors
> small shallow pans

PROCEDURE

To make coffee filter flowers as shown in figure 2.1, add two tablespoons of alcohol and a few drops of one color of food coloring to each shallow pan. This amount is enough to color four large filters, which will make a full flower for one child. Dip several filters into the various colors and allow them to dry. The filters may be cut along the edges to resemble flower petals. Layer them on top of each other in a pleasing design. Pinch the centers together and place a rubber band around the pinched center to create a flower. Add a green pipe cleaner stem and paper leaves if desired.

RECOMMENDATIONS

Use all of the different-colored flowers the children have made and display them in a vase for a beautiful bouquet. Talk about the different kinds of flowers, and see if any of the flowers resemble those in the book by Lobel.

ADDITIONAL EXTENSIONS

Here is another way to make colorful flowers that is reminiscent of the flowers in Ehlert's *Planting a Rainbow*. After discussing warm and cool colors, have children use watercolor paints on card stock to make random blotches of colors. Encourage creative use of the paintbrush to add dots, squiggles, and lines. Mix various colors of green on the card stock also. Allow the paint to dry. Cut or tear out petal or flower shapes from the colors, stem and leaf shapes from the green. Glue on a card stock background folded in a card shape. Children can make a card for a parent, grandparent, or friend by adding a verse.

FIGURE 2.1 ⌒ Coffee Filter Flowers for *Alison's Zinnia*

Barnyard Banter
Denise Fleming (Holt)

Bright handmade paper illustrations accompany the story of noisy farm animals looking for a missing goose. Children will enjoy the rhyme and can help make the animal sounds. The author-illustrator added tiny pieces of actual objects (e.g., grain, grass, straw, stones, etc.) when making the paper for her illustrations.

EXTENSION: **Making Paper**

MATERIALS

tissue or toilet paper	bucket
blender	an iron
warm water	newspaper
wire screen	

PROCEDURE

To make their own paper, have each child choose a piece of tissue to tear into tiny pieces and place in a blender. Add enough warm water to cover the paper. Blend it until it is mushy. As shown in figure 2.2, have two children help pour the pulp onto a screen with a bucket underneath to catch the runoff water. Several children may be involved in holding and, later, emptying this bucket. Give two other children the responsibility of flipping the screen of pulp onto a padding of newspaper. Have children lay additional newspaper on top and then step back as an adult presses the stack with a warm iron to flatten and dry it. Children may carefully peel off the newspaper and allow the paper to finish air-drying. For bright colors, add tempera paint into the pulp.

RECOMMENDATIONS

Try other kinds of paper such as newspaper, construction paper, paper towels, copy paper, recycled greeting cards, stuffing from inside a padded envelope, and so forth. Fleming is a prolific writer with many enjoyable titles children love. In all of her books, she has made her own paper. Share any of her excellent titles.

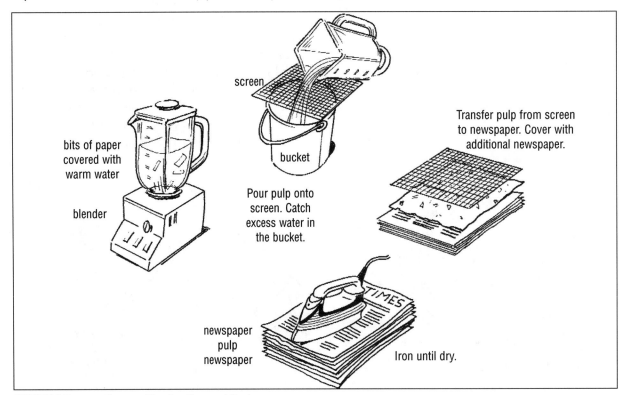

bits of paper covered with warm water

blender

screen

bucket

Pour pulp onto screen. Catch excess water in the bucket.

Transfer pulp from screen to newspaper. Cover with additional newspaper.

newspaper
pulp
newspaper

Iron until dry.

FIGURE 2.2 ~ Papermaking for *Barnyard Banter*

ADDITIONAL EXTENSIONS

This book can be sung using the tune of "Skip to My Lou" for the verses and then shouting out the words for the refrain—"But where's Goose?"

Big Red Bus
Judy Hindley; illustrated by William Benedict
(Candlewick)

The wheel of a big red bus gets stuck in a hole in the road and creates a traffic jam with vans, cars, and a motorcycle until a tractor pulls it out. Repetition and rhythm make this a delightful read-aloud for all ages, including toddlers. The illustrations in this book were executed in ink and gouache.

EXTENSION: Bumpy Road Paint

MATERIALS

> corrugated cardboard
>
> sand
>
> tall, disposable container such as an empty 32 oz. yogurt cup
>
> black tempera paint
>
> yellow or white chalk
>
> glue
>
> paintbrush

PROCEDURE

To make bumpy road paint, allow each child to measure and place a small spoonful of sand in the large disposable container, followed by an equal amount of black tempera paint. Finally, have children add one large squirt of glue to the entire mixture and take turns stirring with a paintbrush (it will be thick). Have children brush the resulting paint on corrugated cardboard to make a bumpy road. When the paint is completely dry, the children may add yellow or white chalk lines to mimic road markings.

RECOMMENDATIONS

You may want to divide the class into groups to save time. The children in one group could add the sand; the next group, the paint; another small group, the dollop of glue; and a final group can stir. All the children could try painting a portion of the road, deciding whether their part will be wide or narrow, curved or straight, an intersection, and so forth. Use all the bumpy paint, or throw the leftovers in the trash rather than rinsing it in a sink, where it may cause drainage problems. Soak the brushes in a pan of water, and dispose of the water in a toilet or other appropriate receptacle.

ADDITIONAL EXTENSIONS

Make a display with the children's roads. They may draw their home next to the road, write their address, add neighbors' houses, and talk about their neighborhood.

Elephant's Wrestling Match
Judy Sierra; illustrated by Brian Pinkney
(Lodestar)

The mighty elephant challenges all the other animals to wrestle with him, but it is only the tiny bat that succeeds in wrestling the elephant to the ground. Pinkney's scratchboard illustrations add to the dramatic retelling of this folktale from Cameroon, Africa.

EXTENSION: Crayon Scratching

MATERIALS

> crayons—bright colors and black or other dark colors
>
> copier paper
>
> magazines for padding
>
> something to scratch off dark colors (any awl-like object, for example, a large paper clip, pen point, etc.)

PROCEDURE

To make their own "scratchboards," have children place a piece of copier paper over a magazine or other padding and color with splashes of bright colors, pressing hard. Then have them color over the bright colors with a black or other dark crayon, also pressing hard. Finally, have them remove the padding and use the scratching instrument to gently scrape away a design or pattern in the dark area to reveal the bright colors beneath.

RECOMMENDATIONS

Use Crayola or other high-quality, waxy crayons for best results. You can purchase commercial scratchboard if you wish, which is what illustrator Pinkney uses.

ADDITIONAL EXTENSION

See if you can make different sounds on homemade or purchased drums. Have children hit the drum on the very edge, near the edge, and then the center. What different sounds occur? See the note on "Talking Drums" in the back of Sierra's book.

Feathers for Lunch
Lois Ehlert
(Harcourt Brace)

A cat escapes from a house through a door mistakenly left open and tries to catch just one of the twelve birds he encounters but only ends up with feathers. Ehlert's brightly colored graphics enhance the text.

EXTENSION: Feather Art

MATERIALS

> construction paper
> feathers
> tempera paint

PROCEDURE

Use a feather as a brush. Have children design their own art by painting with the feather and then cutting out animal shapes if desired. Use one feather for each color of paint and allow the colors to "bleed" together on the paper. You may want to dip an extra feather into water and allow it to drip across the paper to make splotches as Ehlert has done.

RECOMMENDATIONS

Check a chicken or turkey farm for feathers if one is nearby. But caution children not to put these feathers in their mouths and to wash their hands afterward because of health concerns.

ADDITIONAL EXTENSION

Children can also make feather art by gluing feathers onto a mask. Or they can make masks of their own by attaching feathers to one-half of a paper plate and cutting out holes for eye slots. To hold their masks in front of their faces, children may attach a straw or tongue depressor to the mask with glue, tape, or stapling (remember to supervise the stapling).

It Looked Like Spilt Milk
Charles Shaw
(HarperCollins)

Stark white objects centered on bright blue pages have children guessing the identity of each object. Not until the last page do readers discover they are looking at cloud formations.

EXTENSION: Shaving Cream Art

MATERIALS

> blue construction paper (optional)
> shaving cream

PROCEDURE

Squirt shaving cream over a smooth, flat surface such as a table or desk. Children can explore freely, making designs, shapes, animals, and more, much like finger painting. To make a "cloud print," have them put blue construction paper on top of the art, press and rub over the back surface of the construction paper to make a print, and carefully turn the print over and let it dry.

RECOMMENDATIONS

The shaving cream does a wonderful job cleaning dirty desktops! Remember to caution children against ingesting the shaving cream.

ADDITIONAL EXTENSIONS

The idea of using white images on blue paper can be tested with different media. For example, try cotton balls glued on blue paper or a blob of white finger paint spread across the paper with an ice cube, which demonstrates the science concept of melting. Or try torn pieces of white tissue paper or broken eggshells glued to blue paper.

Jubal's Wish
Audrey Wood; illustrated by Don Wood
(Blue Sky)

Jubal sets out one beautiful day to share his feelings of joy with his neighbors but finds that they are not having such a good day. When a wizard grants him one wish, he wishes he could make them happy. It is only after a calamity occurs that his wish is granted. The illustrator used computer-generated art for the illustrations.

EXTENSION: Computer-Generated Art

MATERIALS

computer (multiple computers,
if possible)
color printer (optional)

PROCEDURE

Children take turns adding color and graphics to a blank painting document on the computer and then view the final product. If a printer is available, a copy may be made for display or enough copies made for each child to keep one. If there is a large group of children, they may work together in small groups, or, if working individually, use a timer.

RECOMMENDATIONS

Children especially enjoy using the spray-painting or brush-painting tools, changing the colors, filling shapes with the bucket, and erasing areas. They may also add text to their work.

ADDITIONAL EXTENSIONS

Share another story on wishes, such as the famous folktale "The Three Wishes." Discuss wishes with children. What are their wishes? Have they ever had a wish come true?

Mud
Mary Lyn Ray; illustrated by Lauren Stringer
(Harcourt Brace)

Bright greens, browns, and blues were used to show how the frozen earth in the winter melts and turns into magnificent mud in the springtime. A young boy delights in playing in the mud. The paintings were done with acrylics on watercolor paper.

EXTENSION: Make Mud (Brown Goop)

MATERIALS

1/2 cup cornstarch
1/4 cup water
brown powdered tempera
tray with sides to pour mixture into

PROCEDURE

Have the children help to measure and mix the ingredients together, and let them play with the "mud." Have them describe its feel. Compare it to real mud.

RECOMMENDATIONS

After children have played with the brown goop, save it for the next day and notice how the mixture separates. The bottom layer will feel hard to the touch until it is mixed together again.

ADDITIONAL EXTENSIONS

Use real mud! If you'd like to have children dip their feet in the mud, set up an assembly line of three chairs and three tubs, containing mud, soapy water, and clear water, respectively. Have each child remove a shoe and sock on one foot. Standing in front of the first tub, the child will squish his bare foot in the mud and then make a muddy footprint by stepping on paper. Help him to sit in the first chair, with the soapy-water tub in front of it, to wash his foot. Next, the child moves to the second chair, with the rinse-water tub, and finally to the third chair, with a towel by it, so the child can dry his foot before going to get his shoe and sock. Some children may need help putting the sock and shoe back on.

Olivia Saves the Circus
Ian Falconer (Simon & Schuster)

OR USE

Olivia
by the same author and publisher

Olivia's teacher has her go to the front of the classroom to share a description of her vacation with the class. Olivia always "blossoms" in front of an audience and her story becomes exaggerated with her very vivid imagination. Falconer uses minimalist art with black lines, charcoal shading, white space, and splotches of red in his illustrations.

EXTENSION: **Black-and-White Drawings
with a Hint of Color**

MATERIALS

soft lead pencils   paint

charcoal (optional)   paper

PROCEDURE

Have students discuss why Olivia might have worn red at home and "accessorized" her "really boring uniform" with red. Talk about how the red catches the eye on the otherwise black, gray, and white pages. Have students tell a favorite color of theirs from the rainbow. While students draw a pencil picture of themselves, and color parts of the background dark with their pencils, set up their favorite colors of paint. When they finish their drawings, they may add a touch of that color to their clothing or accessories on their drawing.

RECOMMENDATIONS

Some children will have black, white, or gray as their favorite color. Be prepared with your

response. Either explain that these colors do not appear in the rainbow or on a color wheel and encourage them to choose one that does *or* allow them to skip the painting and compare the effect. Conversely, if children have several favorite colors and cannot decide which to use, you may inform them that warm colors (such as red, orange, and yellow) will seem to come forward more than cool colors (such as green, blue, and violet).

ADDITIONAL EXTENSIONS

Discuss with the students whether Olivia was telling the complete truth about her vacation or stretching the truth. Is it ever OK to embellish our stories? Stretch the truth? Tell a tall tale?

One Potato
Diana Pomeroy (Harcourt Brace)

OR USE

Wildflower ABC
by the same author and publisher

A counting book depicting fruits and vegetables illustrates numbers from one to ten and units of ten to one hundred with potato prints. The author-illustrator used cut potatoes and acrylic paints on felt paper to give a three-dimensional effect to her relief printing.

EXTENSION: **Sponge Prints**

MATERIALS

construction paper

sponge shapes precut with a die-cut
machine or with small, sharp (but-
tonhole) scissors

clothespins

tempera paint (in pans or trays)

PROCEDURE

Have children practice the pincer grip to attach a clothespin to each sponge shape before dipping it into tempera paint. Make prints on construction paper by dabbing the paint-filled sponges as desired across the page.

RECOMMENDATION

To do potato printing, follow the directions at the end of *One Potato*. Because of world hunger and the waste of an edible food, we recommend using sponges instead.

ADDITIONAL EXTENSIONS

This is another opportunity to connect art, literature, and math through the use of patterning. By making a pattern print on large sheets of lightweight paper, children can create their own wrapping paper for gifts. Discuss with your children the patterns they have made. Have they created an *a b a b* pattern or something more complex?

The Party
Barbara Reid
(Scholastic)

Two sisters dread going to their annual family summer party, but once there, they have a wonderful time and do not want to leave. Plasticine artwork is used in the illustrations for this book. The author-illustrator shaped and pressed the plasticine onto illustration board (hot press art board with a quality surface, ideal for illustrations and line work) and used acrylic paint and other materials for special effects.

EXTENSION: **Dough Modeling**

MATERIALS

> 1/2 cup flour
> 1 teaspoon of vegetable oil
> 1/3 cup water
> 2 tablespoons of salt
> 1 teaspoon of cream of tartar
> saucepan
> spoon
> food colors (as desired)

PROCEDURE

Have children help to measure and mix the first five ingredients together. An adult will heat it over a low heat, stirring continuously until it forms a ball. Have children knead the dough when it is cool enough to handle. Then, they may divide it into sections and add one food color to the center of each part and knead to mix that color. Children can make "clay figures." When finished, store leftovers in an airtight container with a lid or a plastic bag that seals. This dough can be reused for at least a year.

RECOMMENDATIONS

You can use any type of modeling dough or fun dough recipe, but we recommend you use one that contains cream of tartar and that is cooked so it stays pliable longer. Or you can purchase commercial modeling compound, for instance, Crayola Model Magic.

ADDITIONAL EXTENSIONS

This book leads to a natural extension—have a party! Let the children help plan a party to be held the next day or week. What games will they play? What food will they eat? Because a cake is an integral part of this story, what type of cake will they have? If you do not want to have a party, have the children describe their family parties. What kinds of food do they normally have? What games do they play?

Planting a Rainbow
Lois Ehlert
(Harcourt Brace)

A young child explains how every year she and her mom plant bulbs in the fall and seeds in the spring, and the end result is a beautiful garden of flowers, all the colors of the rainbow.

EXTENSION: **Rainbow Ladder Book**
MATERIALS

> construction or copier paper in the following colors (one sheet of each color per child): red, orange, yellow, green, blue, purple
> stapler
> tape
> crayons or other coloring materials

PROCEDURE

Older children may do the following independently as you model the procedure, while younger children will need assistance. (The more of the assembly they can do themselves, the more ownership they will feel. Guard against frustration.) Gather a piece each of red, orange, yellow, green, blue, and purple construction paper. Place the red piece of paper vertically on a flat surface and lay the orange piece on top, leaving one-half inch of the red paper showing on the top. Continue in the same manner with the yellow, green, blue, and purple papers, always leaving one-half inch of the previous color showing as in figure 2.3. Keep the sides as even as possible. Holding down the top section of the pages, fold all the bottom sheets up, matching the purple halves on top of each other, with the other pages creating a "ladder" effect. Staple the pages together at the bottom of the folded red sheet. Turn the book around, with the staples at the top. Cover the staples with tape.

Children can draw a flower on each page to correspond with its color.

RECOMMENDATIONS

This book may also be made with half sheets of paper cut horizontally. For an authentic rainbow, a seventh page of indigo, or very dark bluish purple, may be added before the purple page.

ADDITIONAL EXTENSIONS

Have the children help make a rainbow fruit salad with red strawberries, orange slices, yellow pineapple, green grapes, blueberries, and purple plums. For another extension, have children plant bulbs or seeds and label them with the names and colors as presented in Ehlert's book. Watch them grow! See how warthogs mix colors (blue plus yellow equals green, etc.) and create a rainbow at the end of the story in *Warthogs Paint,* by Pamela Duncan Edwards.

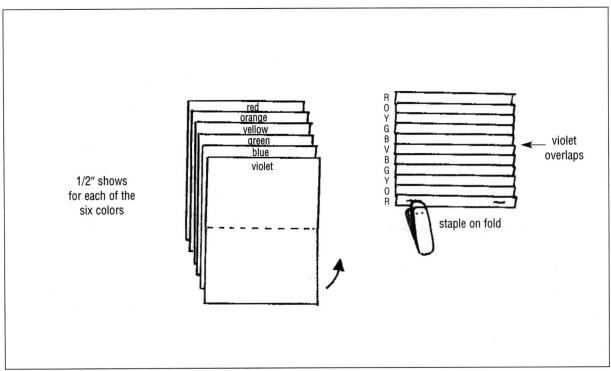

FIGURE 2.3 ～ Ladder Book for *Planting a Rainbow*

Rainbow Fish
Marcus Pfister
(North-South)

A fish with shiny scales decides to share them to make friends with others in the deep blue sea. The bright foil fish scales are particularly appealing to young children.

EXTENSION: **Bubble Wrap Fish Art**

MATERIALS

> construction paper
> bubble wrap that has been cut to fit the size of the construction paper
> blue, green, and bright (fluorescent, if possible) tempera paints

PROCEDURE

To make their own fish with scales, have children lay bubble wrap on a flat surface and coat it with blue or green background paint. Next, they may put a blob of a bright color on top of their background color. Help them press the construction paper on top, rubbing the entire surface of the paper firmly to transfer the paint. When they pull off the construction paper, notice the scale effect as shown in figure 2.4. When the paint is dry, have children cut the paper into a fish shape.

RECOMMENDATIONS

At least two or more prints can be made each time. Add metallic paper or aluminum foil for shiny scales as depicted in the Pfister title.

ADDITIONAL EXTENSIONS

Talk about the fish's attitude at the beginning of the book. He could be described as snobbish. Later, his attitude changed, and he became more understanding of what true friendship means. Did he need to give away his pretty scales to make friends, or was it because his attitude changed? Talk with children about the characteristics of a good friend and why good friends are important. What are some qualities that are not appreciated by others?

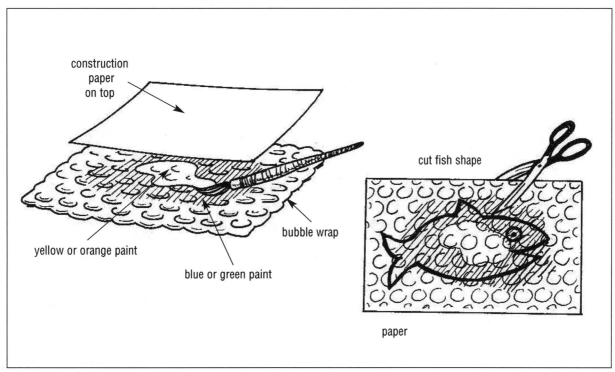

FIGURE 2.4 ~ Bubble Wrap Art for *Rainbow Fish*

Round Trip
Ann Jonas (Greenwillow)

OR USE

Reflections
by the same author and publisher

Read the book the whole way through, and see the sights from the country to the city destination. Then, turn the book upside down, and see the reverse images on the way back from the city to the country. The illustrations in *Round Trip* are executed completely in black and white, while watercolor paintings are used for the reverse images in *Reflections*.

EXTENSION: Mirror Images with Puffy Paint

MATERIALS

> large sheets of construction paper
>
> tempera or poster paint
>
> flour
>
> squeeze bottles (clear, empty shampoo or dish detergent bottles work well)

PROCEDURE

Put paint in a squeeze bottle and add flour by tablespoon to thicken the paint so the colors do not bleed when you make the mirror image. The "puffy" paint will be the consistency of sweetened condensed milk. Have children take turns shaking the bottle so the flour and paint mix together. Have them fold construction paper in half and open it again. Then they squeeze puffy paint on one side only of the opened paper. Press the unpainted side on top of the painted side to make a mirror image.

RECOMMENDATIONS

Puffy paint can be kept for a few days in the refrigerator, but it will soon mold. Do not clog sink drains with this mixture, but it may be flushed down a toilet. If you use disposable squeeze bottles, you can simply discard the paint and container at the same time in the trash.

ADDITIONAL EXTENSIONS

For a language connection, ask children if the resulting art reminds them of anything, and record their responses. For a math connection, have them use Mylar mirrors and set wooden, plastic, or foam pattern blocks up against the mirror to see reflections. Older children could check alphabet letters for horizontal and vertical symmetry. As they hold a mirror up against half of the letter, they can see what happens when the half that shows combines with its reflection. (*See* figure 2.5.)

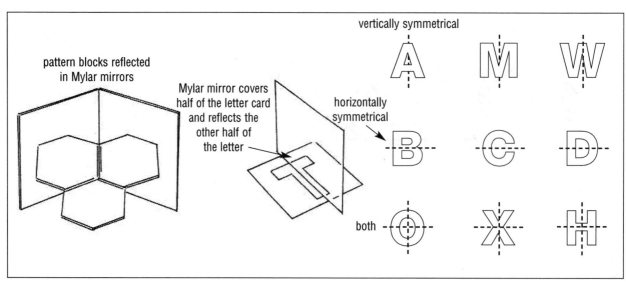

FIGURE 2.5 ～ Letter Symmetry for *Round Trip*

Smoky Night
Eve Bunting; illustrated by David Diaz
(Harcourt Brace)

During a night of rioting in Los Angeles, a young boy and his mother are forced to get along with neighbors they barely knew previously while looking for their lost cats and escaping a fire. Diaz won the Caldecott Medal for his art—acrylic paintings with incredible collage backgrounds that correlate with the text.

EXTENSION: **Object Collage**

MATERIALS

> cardboard or foam trays
>
> tissue paper
>
> materials for collage (beans, seeds, fabric, felt, feathers, etc.)
>
> glue

PROCEDURE

Set out a variety of materials for children to place on cardboard or on a foam tray to form a collage. Have children glue the materials into place when they are satisfied with their arrangement.

RECOMMENDATIONS

Caldecott Medal-winner *Smoky Night* deals with the upheaval during a night of rioting, and the story is probably more suitable for older children, although you can still show the illustrations and explain the procedure of collage to younger children.

ADDITIONAL EXTENSION

In this story, tenants who barely knew each other became friends through an unexpected shared experience. Discuss with your children whether they ever gained a new friend because of unexpected circumstances.

Swamp Angel
Anne Isaacs; illustrated by Paul Zelinsky
(Dutton)

OR USE

The Folks in the Valley
Jim Aylesworth; illustrated by Stefano Vitale
(HarperCollins)

Winner of a Caldecott Honor award, *Swamp Angel* illustrator Zelinsky used oil paints on cherry, maple, and birch veneers to illustrate a modern tall tale with a strong feminine heroine. Swamp Angel, the greatest woods woman in Tennessee, saves settlers and their supplies from the fearsome bear, Thundering Tarnation.

EXTENSION: **Painting on Wood**

MATERIALS

> wood (various shapes and types)
>
> paper
>
> tempera paint or watercolors
>
> twigs and pine needles (optional)
>
> sandpaper (optional)

PROCEDURE

Have children paint on different types of wood. How does the grain of wood affect the colors in their art? Notice the contrast when you use the same type of paint on paper instead of wood. Tempera paint versus watercolor results in a different look on wood also. If you can, have children use both to experiment.

RECOMMENDATIONS

Children can use twigs or pine needles or both for brushes for a different experience. Check with builders, wood shops, or lumberyards for wood scraps. Children enjoy sanding these prior to painting.

ADDITIONAL EXTENSIONS

This story is a modern tall tale. What are some other tall tales that are an important part of U.S.

folklore? Share some other tales—a particularly nice one is *The Bunyans,* by Audrey Wood.

There Was an Old Lady Who Swallowed a Fly
Simms Taback (Viking)

OR USE

Go Away, Big Green Monster!
Ed Emberley (Little, Brown)

Caldecott Medal–winner Taback cleverly illustrates a favorite American folk song. Here children can see inside the old lady's stomach, and die-cut holes increase in size as more animals are eaten. Colorful pieces of torn Kraft (wrapping) paper give a stained glass effect on black endpapers. Throughout the text, mixed media and collage was used on Kraft paper.

EXTENSION: **Die-Cut Stained Glass Art**

MATERIALS

> black construction paper
>
> colored cellophane paper
>
> tape or glue
>
> safety scissors
>
> paper punch (regular or shape or animal punches)

PROCEDURE

Have children fold construction paper in various places (or on angles) and cut out shapes, straight or curly lines, or designs on the fold. When they open the folds, "windows" will be created. They also can use paper punches around the edges for a border. Then have them tape or glue colored cellophane paper on the back for a die-cut stained glass look. Hang the stained glass in a window or where light will shine through the colorful openings.

RECOMMENDATIONS

Children can tear the paper if cutting is too difficult. Also, you can save plastic scraps from a laminating machine and color them with permanent felt-tipped markers instead of using colored cellophane paper.

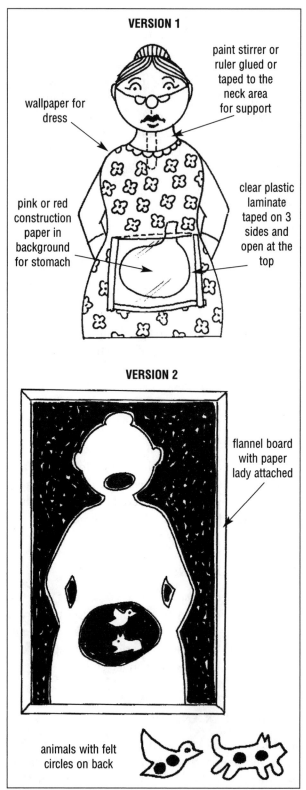

FIGURE 2.6 ~
Figures for *There Was an Old Lady Who Swallowed a Fly*

ADDITIONAL EXTENSIONS

Make an "old lady" out of poster board. Add a ruler or paint stirrer to support the head and as a handle. You can use remnants of wallpaper for her dress. As shown in figure 2.6, use a clear piece of laminate paper and tape over the stomach area, allowing an opening in the top. Make (or have the children make) small animals that correspond with the animals in the story and have children take turns dropping them in her belly as the song is sung. As an alternative, use a paper cutout of the "old lady," and attach it at the top of the head to a flannel board. (*See* figure 2.6.) Drop paper animals with felt circles attached to the back into her cutout mouth. Allow them to fall into her cutout stomach area, and secure them to the flannel board by pushing the felt circles against the background. Make her mouth opening just large enough to accommodate all the animals except the horse, which can get "stuck" in her mouth.

The Very Busy Spider
Eric Carle
(Philomel)

A spider, which is very busy spinning a web, ignores all the farm animals that try to distract her from her work. Children can join in the refrains by making animal sounds and can also feel the spider web being built on each page by touching the raised relief.

EXTENSION: **Raised Relief Art**

MATERIALS

> black construction paper
> glue in squeeze bottles

PROCEDURE

Have children dribble glue on black construction paper to make spider webs or other designs. Let glue harden before touching the raised relief.

RECOMMENDATIONS

Children can also sprinkle colored sand or table salt on top of wet glue for a different raised relief effect. To make colored sand, help them stir a small amount of powdered tempera into the sand or crush colored chalk into the table salt. They may either sprinkle the sand using their pincer grips or shake it on like glitter. Clear glitter may also be used on the wet glue for additional sparkle.

ADDITIONAL EXTENSIONS

Talk about the tactile experience provided with this book and how children who are visually impaired "read" the story with their hands. Provide an example of a Braille book if possible to introduce children to reading with raised dots.

Where Does the Brown Bear Go?
Nicki Weiss
(Greenwillow)

This is a nighttime lullaby with repetitive refrains asking where all the animals go at night. At the end of the story, we find that they are just stuffed animals joining a young boy who is preparing to go to bed. Illustrations are colored pencils on a black background depicting the nighttime scene.

EXTENSION: **Sandpaper Iron Transfer**

MATERIALS

> sandpaper
> wax crayons
> an iron
> brown Kraft (wrapping) paper

PROCEDURE

Have the children draw an animal with crayons on sandpaper and color as desired, pressing very hard. Turn the sandpaper over and place it on top of brown Kraft paper. An adult should iron the back of each piece of sandpaper, using an iron on a low setting (silk) that is just hot enough so the crayon melts onto the brown paper.

Lift the sandpaper off to reveal the reversed image below.

RECOMMENDATIONS

Hang the picture on a window or in front of a light source to see how the art now has a translucent look. Thin Kraft paper and fine-grade sandpaper work best for this art.

ADDITIONAL EXTENSIONS

You can make a mural by having each child make an animal and arranging it on a large piece of Kraft paper. Display the mural on a library or school wall. Have the children tell about their animals.

The Wide-Mouthed Frog
Keith Faulkner;
illustrated by Jonathan Lambert (Dial)

A wide-mouthed frog says to every animal he meets, "I'm a wide-mouthed frog and I eat flies. What do you eat?" until he meets an alligator, who replies that he eats wide-mouthed frogs. Suddenly the frog makes his mouth as small as possible and quickly leaps into the pond with a splash. Numerous pop-out pages of animals' mouths and a surprise pop-up at the end add to the fun.

EXTENSION: **Frog's Mouth Pop-Up Page**

MATERIALS

> construction paper
>
> scissors
>
> decorations for frog's face

PROCEDURE

To make a pop-up frog's mouth, fold green construction paper in half horizontally. Cut a two-inch slit in the middle of the folded edge. Fold the *cut* corners down into triangle shapes as shown in figure 2.7. Unfold the triangles and reverse their direction, pushing them to the inside of the folded paper with a fingertip. Press the triangles into place inside the folded paper. Then hold the paper like a book, and open and close it to make the frog's mouth appear to move.

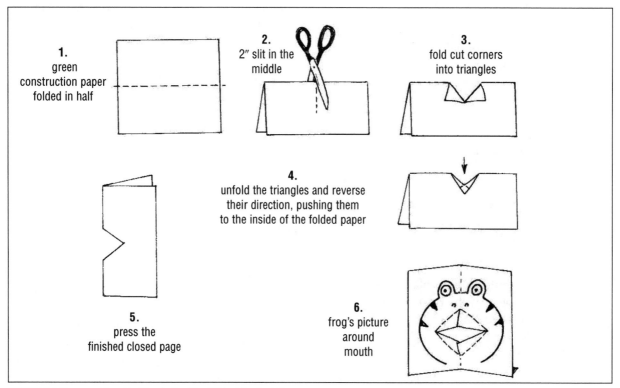

1. green construction paper folded in half

2. 2" slit in the middle

3. fold cut corners into triangles

4. unfold the triangles and reverse their direction, pushing them to the inside of the folded paper

5. press the finished closed page

6. frog's picture around mouth

FIGURE 2.7 ∼ Pop-Up Mouth for *The Wide-Mouthed Frog*

RECOMMENDATIONS

Add wiggle eyes or other decorations and draw around the mouth to finish the frog's head. Older children will be able to make their own frogs. For younger children, demonstrate how to make the frog and then allow the children to take turns manipulating the page and providing the frog's dialogue as he meets each new animal.

ADDITIONAL EXTENSIONS

Sing the song or do the rhyme "Five Green and Speckled Frogs." A recording of this tune entitled "Five Little Frogs" is on Kimbo's *Five Little Monkeys*. Have a frog relay, jumping like frogs from carpet mat to mat, with the carpet mats being lily pads. Arrange the carpet mats in hopscotch order if you want, and have the children count the lily pads as they jump. Share other Faulkner titles such as *The Long-Nosed Pig*.

Note

1. Elizabeth Kelly and Joanne McConville, *Art for the Very Young* (Grand Rapids, Mich.: Instructional Fair/T. S. Denison, 1998), 3.

Bibliography of Picture Books Used in Art Extensions

Aylesworth, Jim. *The Folks in the Valley*. Stefano Vitale, illus. New York: HarperCollins, 1992.

Bunting, Eve. *Smoky Night*. David Diaz, illus. San Diego: Harcourt Brace, 1994.

Carle, Eric. *Very Busy Spider*. New York: Philomel, 1985.

Edwards, Pamela Duncan. *Warthogs Paint: A Messy Color Book*. New York: Hyperion, 2001.

Ehlert, Lois. *Feathers for Lunch*. San Diego: Harcourt Brace, 1990.

_____. *Planting a Rainbow*. San Diego: Harcourt Brace, 1988.

Emberley, Ed. *Go Away, Big Green Monster!* Boston: Little, Brown, 1992.

Falconer, Ian. *Olivia*. New York: Simon & Schuster, 2000.

_____. *Olivia Saves the Circus*. New York: Simon & Schuster, 2001.

Faulkner, Keith. *The Long-Nosed Pig*. Jonathan Lambert, illus. New York: Dial, 1998.

_____. *The Wide-Mouthed Frog*. Jonathan Lambert, illus. New York: Dial, 1996.

Fleming, Denise. *Barnyard Banter*. New York: Henry Holt, 1994.

Hindley, Judy. *Big Red Bus*. William Benedit, illus. Cambridge, Mass.: Candlewick, 1995.

Isaacs, Anne. *Swamp Angel*. Paul Zelinsky, illus. New York: Dutton, 1994.

Jonas, Ann. *Reflections*. New York: Greenwillow, 1987.

_____. *Round Trip*. New York: Greenwillow, 1983.

Lobel, Anita. *Alison's Zinnia*. New York: Greenwillow, 1990.

Pfister, Marcus. *Rainbow Fish*. New York: North-South, 1992.

Pomeroy, Diana. *One Potato*. San Diego: Harcourt Brace, 1996.

_____. *Wildflower ABC*. San Diego: Harcourt Brace, 1997.

Ray, Mary Lyn. *Mud*. Lauren Stringer, illus. San Diego: Harcourt Brace, 1996.

Reid, Barbara. *The Party*. New York: Scholastic, 1997.

Shaw, Charles. *It Looked Like Spilt Milk*. 1947. Reprint, New York: HarperCollins, 1988.

Sierra, Judy. *Elephant's Wrestling Match*. Brian Pinkney, illus. New York: Lodestar, 1992.

Taback, Simms. *There Was an Old Lady Who Swallowed a Fly*. New York: Viking, 1997.

Weiss, Nicki. *Where Does the Brown Bear Go?* New York: Greenwillow, 1989.

Wood, Audrey. *The Bunyans*. David Shannon, illus. New York: Blue Sky, 1996.

_____. *Jubal's Wish*. Don Wood, illus. New York: Blue Sky, 2000.

Bibliography of Musical Recording Used in Art Extension

Various Artists. *Five Little Monkeys*. Long Branch, N.J.: Kimbo, 1999.

Art Resource Books

Brashears, Deya. *Dribble Drabble: Art Experiences for Young Children*. Beltsville, Md.: Gryphon House, 1985.

_____. *More Dribble Drabble: Art Experiences for Young Children*. Orinda, Calif.: Circle Time, 1992.

Carle, Eric. *The Art of Eric Carle.* New York: Philomel, 1996.

_____. *You Can Make a Collage: A Very Simple How-To Book.* Palo Alto, Calif.: Klutz, 1998.

Charner, Kathy, ed. *The Giant Encyclopedia of Art and Craft Activities for Children 3 to 6.* Beltsville, Md.: Gryphon House, 2000.

Hamilton, Leslie. *Child's Play: Easy Art for Preschoolers.* Lincolnwood, Ill.: Contemporary, 1998.

Hodges, Susan. *Toddler Art.* Torrance, Calif.: Totline, 1998.

Kelly, Elizabeth, and Joanne McConville. *Art for the Very Young.* Grand Rapids, Mich.: Instructional Fair/T. S. Denison, 1998.

Kohl, Mary Ann. *Good Earth Art: Environmental Art for Kids.* Bellingham, Wash.: Bright Ring, 1992.

_____. *Mudworks: Creative Clay, Dough, and Modeling Experiences.* Bellingham, Wash.: Bright Ring, 1992.

_____. *Preschool Art: It's the Process Not the Product.* Beltsville, Md.: Gryphon House, 1994.

_____. *Scribble Art: Independent Creative Art Experiences for Children.* Bellingham, Wash.: Bright Ring, 1994.

Lasky, Lila, and Rose Mukerji-Bergeson. *Art: Basic for Young Children.* Washington, D.C.: National Assn. for the Education of Young Children, 1995.

Roche, Denis. *Art around the World: Loo-Loo, Boo, and More Art You Can Do.* Boston: Houghton Mifflin, 1998.

_____. *Loo-Loo, Boo, and Art You Can Do.* Boston: Houghton Mifflin, 1996.

Warren, Jean. *1-2-3 Art: Open-Ended Art Activities for Working with Young Children.* Torrance, Calif.: Totline, 1985.

Chapter Three

Extending Picture Books through Drama

Drama is one of the oldest forms of art in which humans have engaged. From pre-historic times, drama has been an important part of human life. It is also one of the earliest art forms humans perform from birth. An infant imitating sounds and movements is actually acting or dramatizing. Even children playing make-believe, a very natural kind of play, are involved in a form of creative dramatics. Special talent is not necessary—everyone can participate in drama.

STAGES OF PLAY

Early childhood educators have recognized for some time the importance of play in a young child's life. Many books and articles have been written on the subject, and much research has been conducted regarding the value of play. Many parents underestimate play's importance. When evaluating preschool centers for their children, they often look for sites that stress academics rather than those that emphasize play. However, findings indicate that children thrive better in an environment that allows for hands-on experiences and much opportunity for creative play.

There are four natural stages of social development for children in relation to dramatic play.

Solitary Play—Children play totally by themselves. A child who is playing with a doll, feeding it, and talking to it as if she were the mother is involved in solitary play.

Parallel Play—Children are near each other and are engaged in separate play, occasionally imitating the others' actions. The children are cognizant of each other but are not playing together. Their play is independent, and they are unable to be involved yet in the give-and-take of cooperative play.

Associative Play—Children act out their own roles but loosely adopt a play situation of others they are associated with, or in proximity of, while playing. An example is children playing house. The children assume different roles, and they might briefly interact, but they more or less decide and act out their own parts.

Cooperative Play—Children now play with each other and assume roles where they interact with each other. Their play is dependent on others. They are usually acting out an entire story. Children playing school, and interacting with each other while doing this, would be an example of cooperative play.

Preschool- and kindergarten-age children are able to imitate or make sounds presented in stories or to repeat a simple refrain. They can also perform some simple pantomime. When in first grade, they can begin to dramatize simple stories and perform very simple puppetry. By the second or third grade, they can perform improvisation, successfully dramatize stories using simple props and costumes, and perform puppetry or reader's theater.

BENEFITS OF USING DRAMA WITH CHILDREN

Children respond well to dramatic activities for many reasons. The following are just some of the benefits of using drama with children.

- Children have the opportunity to think creatively and develop their imagination.
- They learn to think independently, for example, "How will I act out my role?"
- Drama helps children develop self-esteem.
- It teaches children about social cooperation and group interaction.
- Children learn about group planning and how to have a productive group experience (e.g., the group decides how to perform a scene together).
- Children develop new vocabulary and learn more about written language through acting.
- Acting is a positive way to learn speech patterns and oral expression.
- Drama helps children understand others different from themselves and allows

them to put themselves "in another's shoes."
- Children have the opportunity to release their emotions and use their creative energy.
- Children can become more familiar with good literature.
- Drama is fun for children!

CONSIDERATIONS WHEN USING DRAMA WITH CHILDREN

Not all children are able to perform creative dramatics easily. Some children are self-conscious, others are very shy or timid, some are quiet and have difficulty projecting, and others are show-offs and want to monopolize the "stage." There are children who have short attention spans, and others who are easily distracted. The adult needs to find ways to involve all children, despite these limitations.

It is also important to have plenty of space for children when involving them with drama. Children need to be able to move freely and have room to act out their parts. However, too large of a space can also be problematic. A large gymnasium or meeting room is not always ideal. Voices may echo or distort, and it is hard for young children to project their voices in a large, wide-open space.

SELECTING STORIES FOR DRAMA

What should an adult look for when selecting stories to act out? Here are some points to consider.

- Make sure the story has conflict.
- The story should have action.
- Characters should have distinct personalities.
- There should be strong dialogue that is independent of much description.
- The story should appeal to children.
- There should be a happy ending or one in which vice is punished and virtue

is rewarded. (Young children expect stories to have poetic justice.)

Many of the folk or fairy tales are good for young children to dramatize. Examples are *Goldilocks and the Three Bears, The Three Billy Goats Gruff, Cinderella, The Emperor's New Clothes, The Little Red Hen,* and *The Elves and the Shoemaker.*

DRAMA EXPERIENCES TO USE WITH YOUNG CHILDREN

From storytelling to reader's theater, and from puppetry to magic, there is a wide variety of dramatic experiences for young children. The following drama experiences are ones we selected for our various extensions.

Creative Dramatics

The term *creative dramatics* is typically used to describe the improvised drama of preschool children. Creative dramatics are not practiced but rather spontaneous action and dialogue (if used) that is created by the participants. Nothing is written down, nor do children memorize anything. This is one of the earliest forms of drama that children engage in, and it may last only a few minutes. If you used creative dramatics with a story, the actions would be different each time.

Storytelling with Props and Participation

We use the term *storytelling* very loosely, because true storytelling is done without books, where the teller uses voice and limited action to relay the story. With very young children, however, there is more value in sharing picture book stories, so that they can see the wonderful illustrations. Adding simple props can make the story sharing much more dramatic, particularly for children today, who are more "visual" listeners than children in the past. Moreover, the children can touch or play with the prop later, and many times children will retell the story holding the prop.

Telling Stories through Movement

Stories can be told through movement, for instance, pantomime and improvisation. Dance or music can also extend the story, as indicated in some of our activities below.

Pantomime is a very natural means of expression whereby children act out a character or a part of a story without words but rather through their actions. No sound, props, or objects are used. However, children can use facial expressions, gestures, or other movements in their nonverbal communication.

Unlike pantomime, improvisation is usually based on a story and unfolds as an informal drama. Children may speak, but there is not a script, so no lines need to be memorized. Often the story is made up as children are acting it out, and they determine their own dialogue, movement, and action.

Choral Speaking

Choral speaking is when a group of children read or recite phrases or refrains under the direction of the storyteller. An advantage of choral speaking is that a larger number of children can be engaged. There are five different ways to do choral reading—in unison, antiphonal speaking, cumulative choral speaking, solo choral speaking, and line-around choral speaking.

When the whole group speaks together it is called unison. In antiphonal speaking, children are divided into two groups and each group has its own part. In cumulative choral speaking (which we have used with Eric Carle's *Today Is Monday*), the storyteller has different parts for either individuals or groups of children, and each group (or individual) is added as the story builds. Solo choral speaking allows individual participation, and line-around choral speaking is solo work within the group, with each child being assigned an individual line.

Reader's Theater

Reader's theater is one of the easiest forms of drama to use with elementary-age children. There is no elaborate scenery, costumes and props are not necessary (though sometimes children wear cardboard signs with their characters' names), and, most importantly, children do not need to memorize lines. Actors use their voices rather than movement. The audience uses imagination to picture the setting and the action.

After selecting a piece to use for reader's theater ("Drama Resource Books," at the end of this chapter, lists several books with scripts for children as young as first grade), you may wish to have the children read aloud the script first in round-robin fashion as a group, and then assign parts. The children should practice the script several times until they are familiar with their parts; the adult can help with any pronunciations needed. Next, fasten each script inside a colored folder so that the pages are easy to turn and the audience is not distracted by readers constantly shifting or turning pages. For each individual role, use a bright colored marker to highlight that character's name wherever it appears in the script so that the child will remember when to read. Children can hold their scripts in their hands to perform, but a better method is to have a music stand for each child, and place the script on the music stand. This allows the children to keep their heads up (rather than bending their heads down while reading the script), and their voices will better project out to the audience. If you do not have music stands, tell the children to focus their eyes as often as possible on an object on the back wall (such as a clock) or to focus on two different people, at different angles, near the back of the audience. If you do not want children to stand, they can sit on stools that rotate. When they are not involved in a particular scene, they can rotate in their chairs so their backs face the audience.

The most common problem when children perform reader's theater is to get them to project their voices, but by practicing several times, children gain the confidence to speak more loudly.

Puppets or Masks

The variety of puppets is nearly endless: finger and hand puppets; marionettes; puppets made from paper, sticks, mitts, cups, rods, and handkerchiefs; and shadow puppets, to name just a few. Masks can be made from a wide variety of materials. Puppets and masks can be elaborate or very easy, fun projects for kids to make. Who has not made a spoon puppet at some time?

There are excellent puppets to buy, of course. Folkmanis makes some of our favorites. The quality of these puppets is unmatched, and schools and libraries can buy at a large discount if the puppets are used for educational purposes. To buy just a few, go to their web site, <http://www.folkmanis.com>, and click on the section for buying puppets at Internet stores. Many Internet puppet vendors sell Folkmanis puppets at this site, but we regularly buy from Act II.

Puppet stages can be elaborate (we have made our own out of conduit), but an expensive stage is not necessary. Simply turn a table on its side and cover it with a sheet, or hang a sheet or blanket from a doorway. Or cut a hole in a large carton or box, creating a "stage" where the puppets can perform, or cut a hole in a smaller box and place it on a covered table. Puppeteers sit behind the table and have their puppets perform on the "stage."

Two of our favorite puppet sites are <http://www.puppeteers.org>, the official site of Puppeteers of America, and <http://sagecraft.com/puppetry/index.html>, the Puppetry Home Page, which lists puppet organizations, festivals, information on using puppets, puppet building, performers, and more.

Charades

In charades, one person tries to get an audience to guess a word or phrase by using pantomime. Although young children may need to watch an adult try it first, charades quickly becomes a dramatic activity that engages both the audience and the performers.

Magic

Some readers might not consider magic to be a dramatic activity. However, we feel that a magician deliberately "acts" in a way to try to baffle the audience. Often a costume is involved (a top hat at minimum), the magician needs to practice several times, and sometimes the magician memorizes the "patter" used while performing to distract the audience's attention from any sleight of hand. Thus, magic is a fine fit for a drama extension.

It is now time to be dazzled by some fun drama experiences!

DRAMA EXTENSIONS

Anansi and the Magic Stick
Eric A. Kimmel; illustrated by Janet Stevens
(Holiday House)

Lazy Anansi the spider discovers Hyena's secret to keeping his house so neat—a magic stick. After stealing it, Anansi creates chaos, including flooding the land when he falls asleep after asking the stick to water his plants. All turns out well as the water forms a lake, and the animals build new homes on the lakeshore. Illustrator Stevens used watercolors, watercolor crayons, acrylics, and digital elements to create her colorful, fun illustrations.

EXTENSION: **Magic**

MATERIALS

"magic" stick prop

PROCEDURE

Teach the children the first and last lines of the rhyme—"Hocus-pocus, Magic Stick . . . Quick, quick, quick!"—and have them repeat these words at the appropriate time in the story. Also, add a simple prop—a pencil, a wooden spoon, or such—for a magic stick to wave while telling the story. Then, after consulting several easy nonfiction magic books, teach the children several tricks so they can perform their own magic show. Here are two good magic books with simple tricks—Lawrence Leyton's *My First Magic Book* and *Let's Make Magic,* by Jon Day.

RECOMMENDATIONS

Point out the self-drawn pictures of the author and illustrator on the back end flap of the book. Can the children find these same pictures elsewhere in the book? Mention that illustrators often "hide" personal touches in their illustrations such as their profiles, a picture of their pet, or their name, and so forth.

ADDITIONAL EXTENSIONS

This Anansi tale has similarities to the story of "The Sorcerer's Apprentice," which can be found on the video *Fantasia,* by Walt Disney. Or share another story about magic that gets out of control, such as *Strega Nona,* by Tomie De Paola.

Bark, George
Jules Feiffer
(HarperCollins)

George, a dog, has trouble remembering how to bark, much to his mother's chagrin. After going to the vet, they discover that George can meow, quack, oink, and moo, because of the live animals inside of his stomach. Once the vet removes them, George can again bark until he passes a crowd of people, and then he begins saying "Hello." Feiffer's illustrations appear as cartoons, adding to the hilarity of this simple canine tale.

EXTENSION: **Storytelling with Props**

MATERIALS

stuffed animal dog
small beanbag cat
small beanbag duck
small beanbag pig
small beanbag cow
lingerie laundry bag or garbage bag
poster board
colored markers

PROCEDURE

Ahead of time, the storyteller prepares four poster board speech balloons as shown in figure 3.1.

FIGURE 3.1 ~ Materials for *Bark, George*

Each poster board sign should have an animal sound on it for the cat, duck, pig, and cow as given in the book (Meow, Quack, Oink, and Moo). Next, attach a small lingerie laundry bag to the reverse side of a table, so that children do not see it, and place the dog on the table. Add the beanbag animals to the bag in the order they appear in the story. When telling the story, hold up the speech balloon signs at the appropriate time so that the children can make the animal sound. When the vet reaches in the dog's mouth and pulls out the animals one by one, the storyteller pretends to reach down the dog's mouth and pulls out the animals one by one. This is a great example of a participation story with props.

RECOMMENDATIONS

If you do not have access to a large stuffed dog, you may use a smaller one and place it on a table that has a tablecloth or an overhanging cover to hide the bag attached to the back of the table. Work from behind the table to retrieve the animals from the dog's "mouth."

ADDITIONAL EXTENSION

Share the book *Martha Speaks,* by Susan Meddaugh, or any of her other titles about Martha, a dog that speaks like a human after eating vegetable soup. Then, have the children make sock puppet dogs. For each child you will need a knee-high sock for the body, a piece of oval-shaped poster board folded in half for the mouth, two ears, and buttons for the nose and eyes. Slide the folded poster board inside the sock for the mouth, and then have each child try on the sock to mark where the nose and eyes should be. Hot glue the buttons in place, and add the ears. Children then slide their hands inside the socks with their fingers on top of the folded poster board and their thumbs on the bottom to make their dogs "speak." Then have the children talk like Martha or George.

Cinderella's Rat
Susan Meddaugh
(Houghton Mifflin)

This story's narrator is a rat that was turned into a coachman by Cinderella's fairy godmother. His sister rat accompanies him to the castle, and when another boy tries to kill her, a series of misunderstandings and magical spells will keep children thoroughly amazed. At the end, the coachman narrator turns back into a rat at midnight, but his sister remains a human. The animated art only adds to the wit and cleverness of this twisted Cinderella tale.

EXTENSION: Improvisation

MATERIALS

PROCEDURE

Before presenting a twisted tale, make sure the children are very familiar with the original version. Prior to sharing *Cinderella's Rat,* have children retell the folktale *Cinderella* by acting out the parts without a script. This is an example of improvising a known tale. First, ask children to name the characters; then, assign parts to volunteers. Extra children can be attendees at the ball. After this performance, share the twisted version, *Cinderella's Rat.* Talk with children about how elements of the original tale are sustained in this newer rendition.

RECOMMENDATIONS

You may want to add props when children are improvising the original tale. Add a broom, a clear plastic shoe with sparkles, a pumpkin, and ragged and dress-up clothing.

ADDITIONAL EXTENSIONS

There are many other versions of the Cinderella tale from around the world. Some of our favorites are *Cendrillon,* by Daniel San Souci; *Mufaro's Beautiful Daughters,* by John Steptoe; *The Rough-Face Girl,* by Rafe Martin; *Yeh-Shen,* by Ai-Ling Louie; *Cinderella,* by Diane Goode; and *The Korean Cinderella,* by Shirley Climo. Share some of these variants, and then chart the similarities and differences between the tales. Do they begin and end the same way? Are there clues that help establish the origin of the tales and the different countries represented? Are the details related to the transformations similar? Compare the illustrations of the various picture books. Then have children vote on their favorite rendition.

Duck in the Truck
Jez Alborough
(HarperCollins)

A duck driving a truck gets stuck in the muck. A frog, a sheep in a jeep, and a goat try to help him get out and only succeed with the help of a rope and motorboat. The duck continues on his travels, unaware that the frog, sheep, and goat are still stuck in the muck. The playful rhyme and large animated illustrations add to the lively romp.

EXTENSION: Telling a Story through Movement

MATERIALS

brown Kraft (wrapping) paper (optional)

PROCEDURE

There are four characters in this story—a duck, a sheep, a frog, and a goat. Assign parts and have the children come to the front of the room. While telling the story, have each character come forward and help push the truck, as in the story. The truck can be imaginary, but the child should be told to push very hard. You can use brown Kraft paper on the floor to represent the muck. Or make this story into a participatory tale by having children add the extra words "in the muck" both times the phrase "the truck still stuck" appears in the text. Tell children to listen carefully for those words, and, as the storyteller, make sure you emphasize them. Also, at the end of the story, let them again supply the three words "in the muck" after you say the word "stuck."

RECOMMENDATIONS

If you want all the children involved, here are two ideas. Divide participants into four groups, and have the ducks, the frogs, the sheep, and the goats pushing the truck at the appropriate time. Or use some of the children as props, assigning some volunteers to become the truck, one to be the rock, and several to be the vegetables in the back of the truck, which fly out when the truck bumps on the rock and becomes stuck. Continue in this way for the other characters and props, such as the jeep, until all children have participated. If you have many children and need more assigned parts, add the jeep and the truck as additional roles.

ADDITIONAL EXTENSION

Do an entire program on mud! Examples are the book *Mud,* by Mary Lyn Ray (found in chapter 2), and Lynn Plourde's *Pigs in the Mud in the Middle of the Rud* (included in this chapter below).

Fat Cat
Margaret Read MacDonald;
illustrated by Julie Paschkis
(August House Little Folk)

This variant of a traditional Danish folktale details the antics of a very hungry cat that eats everything in his sight, including his friend the mouse. The mouse uses her scissors, which were also swallowed, to snip open the cat's stomach so that all can escape but then uses her needle and thread to sew him back up. The vivid gouache paintings appear as folk art, fitting for this cumulative tale.

EXTENSION: Acting Out a Story with Props

MATERIALS

> a king-sized sheet
>
> cat ears
>
> safety scissors

PROCEDURE

Assign the following parts to children: cat, mouse, washerwoman, soldiers, king, and elephant. Have the cat wear ears, and drape the sheet around the child's shoulders. Then, read the story and have the cat "swallow" the characters as given in the story. The cat "swallows" them at the appropriate time by enveloping them in the sheet and hiding them from the audience so that the cat appears to become fatter. The children who are "gobbled up" scrunch down under the sheet. Props can be imaginary, but we like to have the mouse hold child's scissors so that when the characters pop out from under the sheet near the end of the story, the mouse can triumphantly hold up

her scissors. This extension involves storytelling with limited props, creative drama, and simple pantomime.

RECOMMENDATIONS

Use any color sheet for the cat. A white sheet would be a white cat, a black sheet a black cat, or an orange or yellow sheet would keep the appearance of the illustrated cat in the story. We do not use many props for this story, but have the cat simply swallow imaginary swords and so forth. However, you may want to add poster board props.

ADDITIONAL EXTENSION

Use the classic children's song "The Cat Came Back" and have children join in the refrain. It is a fun song to sing with children, but the adult should be prepared to discuss why cruelty to animals should never occur and that there are homes for unwanted animals. Dean Wilson performs one of our favorite versions of this song on *A Child at Heart.* Some verses in this song may be objectionable because of violence, especially in light of current circumstances in our world. We find the Wilson version acceptable, but be certain to preview whatever version of this song you use.

Five Little Monkeys Sitting in a Tree
Eileen Christelow
(Clarion)

Five little monkeys and their mother head to the river for a picnic supper. While Mama snoozes, the little monkeys climb a tree to tease a crocodile. One by one they disappear, to their mother's frantic desperation, but alas, they are safe hiding in the tree. The traditional rhyme is accompanied by colored pencil drawings.

EXTENSION: Creative Drama with Motions

MATERIALS

> none

PROCEDURE

This is a perfect story for a creative drama experience with motions. Read the story and have the children hold up the correct number of fingers each time to represent the monkeys and then lay them on their opposite arms to represent the tree branch. Next, they can stick their thumbs in their ears and wiggle their fingers to tease the crocodile while using a high-pitched voice to mock him saying, "Can't catch me!" Have them extend their arms in front as the crocodile's jaw and snap them each time the crocodile snaps his jaw in the story.

RECOMMENDATIONS

Christelow currently has four other books about the five little monkeys (*see* "Bibliography of Picture Books Used in Drama Extensions" at the end of this chapter). Several of them are very adaptable to act out with motions or creative drama. For example, *Five Little Monkeys Jumping on the Bed* lends itself well to active motion.

ADDITIONAL EXTENSIONS

For a musical version of *Five Little Monkeys Jumping on the Bed* that children can act out and sing along to, consult the *Five Little Monkeys* recording by Kimbo. For a flannel board presentation of other stories about monkeys and crocodiles, refer to *The Flannel Board Storytelling Book*, by Judy Sierra, listed under "Drama Resource Books" at the end of this chapter. Two different stories given in it would make good extensions: "Counting Crocodiles" is a tale from Indonesia, and "The Monkey and the Crocodile" is an Indian tale. Hand out the pieces of the story and have children bring them up and place them on the flannel board as you tell the story.

Going to the Zoo
Tom Paxton; illustrated by Karen Lee Schmidt
(Morrow)

Paxton's classic children's song of Daddy taking his young children to the zoo even depicts the animals in the illustrations singing along. Dad is exhausted after the experience, but Mom dons her circus hat and sets the alarm to get up early the next morning to take the kids again. The musical score is contained on the end pages. Illustrator Schmidt uses watercolor and gouache for the fun-loving illustrations.

EXTENSION: **Animal Movements to Music**

MATERIALS

> tape or CD player
> musical recording of "Going
>   to the Zoo"

PROCEDURE

Sing the story first so that children are familiar with the music and the words. Then play a musical recording of the song and have the children act out the different animal movements as given in the text. Children can sing the refrain and make appropriate motions by clapping on the first and last line of the refrain, pointing to other children on the second line, and motioning to "come along" on the third line. Two of our favorite recordings of this piece are by the song's creator, Paxton, on *The Marvelous Toy* and the version by Peter, Paul, and Mary on the album titled *Peter, Paul, and Mommy*. This activity is an example of pantomime.

RECOMMENDATIONS

Neither recording listed above follows the text exactly. The librarian or teacher must play the tape before presenting the book to see which pages are different. We paper clip the pages together for the verses in the text that are not on the recording so that the story flows with the music. The *Peter, Paul, and Mommy* recording actually follows the book more closely than the recording by the author.

ADDITIONAL EXTENSIONS

Talk about the different animals you see at the zoo and discuss their habits, how they move, and what they eat. Fasten a large piece of mural paper or Kraft (wrapping) paper to the wall and have the children use markers to draw different zoo animals as a backdrop for their performance. Then, hold a zoo party and serve peanuts (elephant), bananas (monkey), and goldfish crackers (seals).

Goldilocks and the Three Bears
Valeri Gorbachev
(North-South)

The traditional fairy tale is accompanied by child-appealing illustrations and modern-day details such as large gold hoop earrings worn by Mama Bear, flip-flops worn by Dad, and pink tennis shoes worn by Baby Bear. Goldilocks is portrayed as a small, innocent child who simply stumbled upon the homey cottage.

EXTENSION: **Pantomime**

MATERIALS

PROCEDURE

First, share the traditional story of the three bears. Then, put the book down, and have the children pantomime the actions of the lead character, Goldilocks. Tell the children what Goldilocks does, but do not have them speak; rather, they should just act out the story. Goldilocks peeks through the window, opens the door and goes inside, smells the porridge, and tastes all three bowls, making appropriate facial and body expressions to indicate the porridge temperature. Then, as Goldilocks, they should try all three chairs and all three beds, again making appropriate movements to coincide with details of the story. At the end, Goldilocks jumps out the window and runs away through the forest.

RECOMMENDATIONS

Watch for the children's actions as you retell the story to see what they devise. Some of their actions may be exaggerated, which adds to the fun of the pantomime. They may hold their hands above their brows to shield their eyes as they peer through the window, sniff deeply for the smell of

the porridge, shiver violently for the cold porridge, and fan their tongues vigorously for the hot.

ADDITIONAL EXTENSION

This book lends itself well to the math concepts of number, size, and one-to-one correspondence. Provide props of large, medium-sized, and small bowls, spoons, chairs, and bed coverings for the children to compare and sort into the order given in the story. Reread the story and have the children use these props appropriately. Use a deep, normal, or high voice for each of the bears, and encourage the children to join in with you.

Goldilocks and the Three Hares
Heidi Petach
(Putnam)

A twisted variant of the traditional classic folktale, this version features hares instead of bears. A play-within-a-play with mice as the commentators adds to the fun. Equally humorous balloon dialogues accompany the hilariously detailed illustrations of the elaborate hare's hole in the ground.

EXTENSION: **Reader's Theater**

MATERIALS

typed scripts
highlighter
colored file folders (optional)

PROCEDURE

The text of this book can easily be made into reader's theater scripts for children to perform by deleting the dialogue in the borders for the mice, moles, and weasels. Without those sections, the storyteller has a wonderful twisted version of *Goldilocks and the Three Bears*. First, type the text of the script into a reader's theater format (like a play script with the character name and colon followed by the spoken parts). All the text that is not written in a speech balloon is added to the narrator's part. Then, type the spoken parts (speech balloons) for each remaining character: Father, Mother, Baby, Goldie, and Police. After typing one script, print six copies (one master copy and six performer scripts). Then hand label each script with its character's name. Go through each script to highlight that character's name so that the child will quickly see her or his speaking parts. Staple each script inside a file folder for a more professional appearance. Drama experiences include both reader's theater and making a play from a story.

RECOMMENDATIONS

Share the book before doing the reader's theater version so that children are acquainted with the story. Also, children can then see the additional activity and dialogue by the moles, mice, and weasels and references to the author and illustrator that are not part of the scripted play.

ADDITIONAL EXTENSION

Children of all ages enjoy the "Three Bears Rap" or "Three Bears Chant." Our favorite recording of this can be found on *Music Mania*, by Stephanie K. Burton. This chant-rap is perfect for the musical concept of keeping the beat. Young children can clap their hands or tap their thighs to the beat, and older children, with developed fine-motor abilities, can snap their fingers to the beat. On this recording, the performer makes a jazzy hissing sound that children will enjoy imitating.

The Hat
Jan Brett
(Putnam)

Lisa hangs her woolen clothes on the clothesline outside to air them, but one stocking falls off the line. A curious hedgehog gets the stocking stuck on his prickles, and all the other animals laugh at him. Hedgie leads them to believe that a hat is the thing, and they all run off to get their own hats. Meanwhile, Lisa is shown in borders on each page getting ready for winter until she realizes her stocking is missing and reenters the story looking for it. Author-illustrator Brett traveled to Den-

mark to make her glorious paintings so that they would accurately portray a Scandinavian farm.

EXTENSION: **Storytelling with Props**

MATERIALS

> an assortment of hats or articles
> of winter clothing

PROCEDURE

Share the story first so that children understand the plot and the fact that Hedgie mistakenly got a wool sock stuck on his head. Next, for the extension, have children retell the story with an adult reading most of the story except for the animals' questions and Hedgie's responses. For ease of memorization, have each child portraying an animal ask the same question, "What's that on your head, Hedgie? You look funny!" or a variation of this question. For Hedgie's spoken responses, have cards typed up with the different responses given in the book. If they are placed in order as given in the book, the child playing Hedgie can just turn the cards over and respond in order. Then, a child playing Lisa can say her two lines about how ridiculous Hedgie looks. Near the end of the story, all the children portraying animals can reappear with their hats or winter clothing articles on their heads while Hedgie responds with the last line of the story. Drama experiences include storytelling with props and making a play from a story.

RECOMMENDATIONS

Point out to the children during the first reading that the illustrations that surround the text as a border tell their own story. They show Lisa preparing for winter as her clothes disappear from the clothesline. Children can then predict what will happen next in the story by seeing an animal on the right-hand border of one page that will then reappear on the following page.

ADDITIONAL EXTENSION

Share Brett's book *The Mitten* for another animal story that takes place in the winter and has exciting and predictive action in the borders. Prepare a large laminated paper mitten "envelope" and paper animals from the story. Assign two children to hold the top edges of this mitten, and distribute the characters to other children. As the story is reread, children take turns dropping the various-sized characters into the large mitten until it is filled and "bursts" open at the end. If you have access to someone who works with yarn, procure a knitted or crocheted white mitten (fashioned with large needles or a thick hook) that will stretch. For a wealth of ideas on using all of Brett's books, including patterns for the paper animals for *The Mitten* and animal masks and a script for *The Hat* and much more, see her web site, <http://www.janbrett.com>.

Hattie and the Fox
Mem Fox; illustrated by Patricia Mullins
(Simon & Schuster)

Hattie sees first a nose, then eyes, then ears, then a body, then legs, and finally a tail in the bushes and finally figures out it is a fox. The other animals react nonchalantly until Hattie shouts out, "It's a fox!" The cow's loud "moo" fortunately scares the fox away. Mixed-media illustrations accompany this very simple tale.

EXTENSION: Choral Reading

MATERIALS

cue cards

PROCEDURE

Prepare cue cards for each animal (goose, pig, sheep, horse, cow) except for Hattie, the hen, and the fox. The narrator can be Hattie and read her lines along with extraneous text. The fox has a nonspeaking part and needs only to "jump out" of the "bushes" at the appropriate place in the text. Cue cards can be made by an adult for the other animals in the story, writing the two phrases each animal says in the text on the individual cue cards. The first phrase each animal says is repeated five times. Tell children they will repeat the first phrase on their cue card five times, and

they will repeat the last phrase only once, after Hattie says she sees a fox. If you have a large group of children, several can be geese, pigs, sheep, horses, and cows and read their lines together. Drama experiences used are choral reading and line-around choral speaking.

RECOMMENDATIONS

For younger children, teach them their repeating line and then allow them to improvise their own reaction to the news, "It's a fox!"

ADDITIONAL EXTENSIONS

In addition to being an excellent story to use as a choral reading, this can also be acted out as a puppet play, because the lines would be easy to memorize. For simple costuming ideas, consult the puppet-making books in "Drama Resource Books" at the end of the chapter for ideas about making character puppets for each animal involved in the story. Suggestions are stick puppets or paper-bag puppets. Another story to share at the same time as this one with a similar theme is *Henny Penny,* by Jane Wattenberg. This story can also be performed easily.

The Little Red Hen
Paul Galdone
(Clarion)

A classic version of the traditional tale of the little red hen who ends up doing all the housework while her housemates the mouse, cat, and dog all nap. Galdone has placed his characters in an abandoned farmhouse and used rustic colors and lighthearted characterizations to delight young children.

EXTENSION: Body Bag Puppets

MATERIALS

large grocery bags
various colors of poster board
stapler or hot glue gun
wiggly eyes

chenille stems

grosgrain ribbon

feathers

cat and dog collars (optional)

PROCEDURE

This story is fun to act out with body bag puppets as shown in figure 3.2. To make these, use large paper grocery bags for each character (the little red hen, the mouse, the cat, and the dog). Staple or hot glue appropriate poster board colors (red for the hen, etc.) to a closed grocery bag turned upside down. One piece of poster board will be attached to the flap and the other piece beneath the flap of the bag (as in a paper bag puppet). Have children glue on chenille whiskers, wiggly eyes, feathers for the hen, and real cat and dog collars (or make those out of poster board), and add other details as desired. Finally, fasten grosgrain ribbon to the top center of the back of the puppet so that the body bag can be tied around a child's neck. The bag is never opened; rather, it lies flat against the child's body, and the character puppet is actually hanging from the child's neck.

To act out the story, the reader plays the part of the little red hen and holds the book with one hand while reading the story and acting out the movements with the other hand while also reading the narrator parts. Children are told ahead of

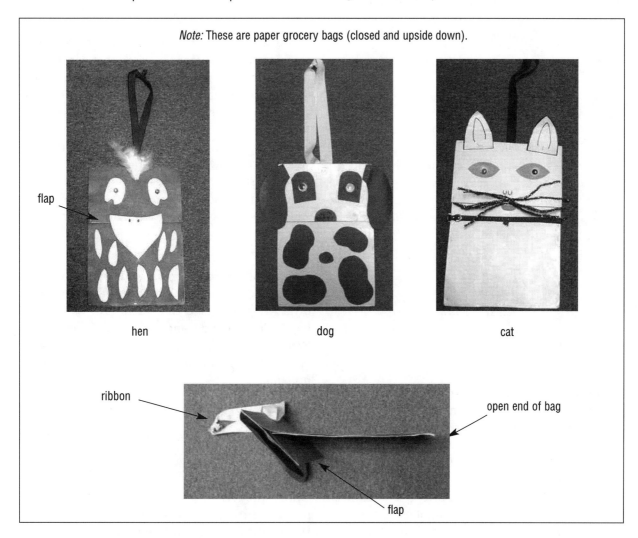

Note: These are paper grocery bags (closed and upside down).

flap

hen　　　　　dog　　　　　cat

ribbon

open end of bag

flap

FIGURE 3.2 ~ Puppets for *The Little Red Hen*

time that they will be prompted for their lines. For example, the narrator will say, "The mouse said . . ." and will then pause each time while the child assuming the role of the mouse responds, "Not I." All of the characters respond this way every time except when the narrator asks, "Who will eat this cake?" at which time their response is an enthusiastic, "I will!" Children can also add movements according to the narration. Drama experiences for this book include making puppets and acting with puppets.

RECOMMENDATION

It is not always possible to get large grocery bags at stores. If you have difficulty finding them, check with a restaurant supply house or order them from craft catalogs.

ADDITIONAL EXTENSIONS

Once children are familiar with the original tale, share two twisted versions that are a lot of fun. Janet Stevens and Susan Stevens Crummel have written a tale titled *Cook-a-Doodle-Doo!* and Philemon Sturges has another variant with his story *The Little Red Hen (Makes a Pizza)*. For a flannel board version of *The Little Red Hen,* consult Judy Sierra's *The Flannel Board Storytelling Book* (listed under "Drama Resource Books" at the end of this chapter).

Master Man
Aaron Shepard;
illustrated by David Wisniewski
(HarperCollins)

Shadusa believes he is the strongest man in the world and tells his wife Shettu to call him Master Man. Shettu warns him not to boast, saying there will always be someone stronger, and, sure enough, there is not one but two other Master Men. It is these two men fighting to see who is the strongest that creates thunder, according to this Nigerian tale. Caldecott-winning illustrator Wisniewski adds elaborate cut-paper illustrations in a comic-book format.

EXTENSION: **Reader's Theater**

MATERIALS

scripts

PROCEDURE

The author of this book has reader's theater scripts of the story at his web site, <http://www.aaronshep.com/rt/RTE27.html>. Print the scripts for the performance and assign parts. While performing, children can also pantomime the actions, particularly if the scripts are on music stands (as suggested above). Have the child who plays the role of the baby sit on the floor.

RECOMMENDATIONS

If you have access to Body Sox (a very stretchy, translucent pillowcase-like sack that closes over the entire body), the two children playing the roles of the two largest Master Men can each wear one. (You can order Body Sox from the Music in Motion catalog, mentioned in chapter 4.) Download and print the character posters from the web site, <http://www.aaronshep.com/extras/index.html#MasterMan>, and fasten each of the Master Men's heads to an empty cardboard roll from gift wrap. Have the children hold them in place.

ADDITIONAL EXTENSIONS

This tall tale is from Nigeria, and you may want to share other tall tales. Two of our favorites about other larger-than-life characters are *The Bunyans,* by Audrey Wood, and *Sally Ann Thunder Ann Whirlwind Crockett,* by Steven Kellogg. These tales, like *Master Man,* explain the origin of natural phenomena.

Piggie Pie!
Margie Palatini; illustrated by Howard Fine
(Clarion)

Gritch the Witch decides she wants to make piggie pie to eat but is frustrated to realize that she is missing the most important ingredient—pigs! Flying on her broom to Old MacDonald's farm, she soon discovers there are no pigs to be found. Unbeknownst to her, the pigs all donned animal costumes. Palatini incorporates verses of the song "Old MacDonald" to add more "oomph" to this highly amusing tale, which is accompanied by illustrations rendered in pastels.

EXTENSION: **Participation Story**

MATERIALS

>   pink poster board
>   yellow poster board
>   colored marker

PROCEDURE

Make two pink poster board signs. On the first write in large letters the words "Piggie Pie." Turn it over and write "No Piggies" on the other side. On the second piece of poster board write "No Problem," and flip it over to write "Problem" on the opposite side. On the yellow piece of poster board write "Old MacDonald's Farm; Call Ei-Ei-O; Just over the River and through the Woods; We Have Ducks, Chickens, and PIGGIES!" as given in the illustration of the "Yellow Pages" found in the book. Then, the storyteller relates the story and holds up the correct sign for the children to say the lines, pausing to let them complete the phrase. This is an excellent way for children to get involved in the storytelling with participation as a drama experience.

RECOMMENDATIONS

This is a perfect story to share with a large group of children. If they cannot see the book, the storyteller can lay it on a table and tell the story, leaving both hands free to hold up the signs. When telling the story, you will need to describe the double-page spread when the pigs are donning their costumes because the story has no text for this part. Also, if telling the story and not holding up the book, explain within the story that when Gritch shouts to an animal, the animal is actually a pig in an animal costume. We normally whisper that unwritten part to build suspense and because it is to be kept secret from Gritch. For

example, when Gritch shouts to a duck, whisper, "Who was really a pig in a duck costume!" Make sure you practice the story before presenting it so that you know when to hold up the signs. We always sing the part in the story that correlates to the "Old MacDonald" song.

ADDITIONAL EXTENSIONS

When Gritch meets the wolf, he states that he has been chasing "three little pigs for days." Ask the children what story this refers to. Then, share the story of *The Three Little Pigs* (*see* Barry Moser's version below), or share the song "Who's Afraid of the Big Bad Wolf?" on the recording *Four Baby Bumblebees,* and have children sing along with the familiar refrain.

Pigs in the Mud in the Middle of the Rud
Lynn Plourde; illustrated by John Schoenherr
(Blue Sky)

Because of heavy rains, a Model T Ford gets stopped in the road by some pigs playing in the mud. Grandma shouts to the other occupants in the car about the obstacle, and Brother tries to shoo them away, to no avail. Other animals join the muddy mess while more family members try to chase them away. Grandma finally clears the scene, though she, too, ends up in the mud. Earth colors predominate in the line drawings of the farm animals and family.

EXTENSION: **Choral Speaking**

MATERIALS

>   none

PROCEDURE

Teach the children the refrain "Oh no. Won't do. Gotta shoo. But who?" which repeats five times. They may have difficulty remembering the words the first time, but show children that by adding motions to the phrases, it becomes easier to remember the words. For example, for "Oh no," they can lightly hit the palm of one hand along the side of their head. For "Won't do," they can waggle an index finger back and forth. "Gotta shoo" may be performed by moving their hands in a modified breaststroke motion. For "But who?" arms may be outstretched with palms facing upward. This allows for the drama experience of choral speaking in unison.

RECOMMENDATIONS

For Grandma's lines, the storyteller should use a loud voice or make a calling-out motion by placing both hands alongside of her mouth and shouting out the lines. Also, discuss what the word *rud* means. In a New England dialect, the word *road* is pronounced "rud."

ADDITIONAL EXTENSION

Share another book about animals that love mud puddles, in this case pigs, in the story *The Piggy in the Puddle,* by Charlotte Pomerantz. This story also contains silly rhyming words and is fun to share.

The Three Billy Goats Gruff
Paul Galdone
(Clarion)

Another of author-illustrator Galdone's renditions of classic animal nursery tales, this one has particularly large, bold double-spread pages, which makes it an excellent choice for group story time. Particularly effective are the pages depicting the largest Billy Goat Gruff crossing the bridge; he literally leaps out at the reader. Though this is an older book, it still remains a superior choice for this traditional tale.

EXTENSION: Acting Out a Story with Puppets and Music

MATERIALS

> small white paper bag
>
> medium-sized paper bag
>
> two large grocery bags
>
> poster board
>
> crepe or tissue paper
>
> yarn or string

> colored markers
>
> grosgrain ribbon
>
> stapler
>
> tape or CD player
>
> musical recording of "The Three Billy Goats Gruff"

PROCEDURE

Children will use puppets for the goats and troll and act out the story from the book or to the song "The Three Billy Goats Gruff" by Greg and Steve on their recording *Greg and Steve Rockin' Down the Road.* Encourage children to join in the refrain, "Trip, Trap, Trip, Trap, Trip, Trap." As shown in figure 3.3, use a small white paper bag for the small billy goat, and a medium-sized paper bag for the middle billy goat. (A deli may have these two different sizes.) For the large billy goat and the troll, use large grocery bags. For all three goat puppets add poster board ears and use colored markers for facial features. Snip crepe or tissue paper to make a "goatee" on each. For the troll, add string or yarn hair, and use strips of crepe or tissue paper for the fur. Then, either cut out eyeholes for children to wear the larger grocery bags as head coverings or follow the directions under Paul Galdone's *Little Red Hen* above and attach grosgrain ribbon. Drama experiences include storytelling with music, making puppets, and creative drama.

RECOMMENDATIONS

The children will most likely be happy to help make the goat masks. Have them step on poster board with the arches of their feet along the edge and trace around their heels. Cut out the resulting half ovals to use as goat ears. If you have access to a wooden classroom boat that could be flipped over to form a bridge, use the bottoms of the seats and floorboards as steps and the curved part as the arch of the bridge.

ADDITIONAL EXTENSION

The story can also be presented as a panel theater production. (*See* figure 3.4.) Directions for making

small billy goat
paper bag puppet

middle billy
goat mask

large billy
goat mask

troll mask

FIGURE 3.3 ~ Puppets and Masks for *The Three Billy Goats Gruff*

a panel theater are in Connie Champlin's book, *Storytelling with Puppets,* listed in "Drama Resource Books" at the end of this chapter. The storyteller may make the theater ahead of time, or the children may help with this project as time permits. Attach three rectangles of blue poster board together with tape along their shorter sides to form a panel with three parts. This will serve as both the background of sky as well the water under the bridge. Add cut green paper as grass to the left and right side panels, with the grass on the left panel short and sparse and that on the hill of the right panel longer and lush. Draw a bridge shape that spans the middle panel and an

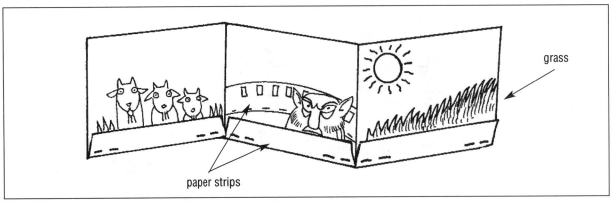

FIGURE 3.4 ~ Panel Theater for *The Three Billy Goats Gruff*

optional sun in the sky for the right panel. Staple a narrow strip of poster board along the bottom of the entire panel so poster board cutouts of each character may be inserted into it and moved across the panels to show the actions of the story. Also add a paper strip to the bridge to move the goats across it. Place the three goats into the strip on the left panel and the troll on the middle panel to begin the story. By the end of the story, the three goats will have crossed over the bridge to the right side, and the troll will be gone.

The Three Little Pigs
Barry Moser
(Little, Brown)

Moser relates the classic tale of the three little pigs that set off in the world to seek their fortune and build their own houses, but the details in the watercolor illustrations are particularly modern and somewhat irreverent, though very humorous for older children. The wolf, who has just dined on pig, wipes his chin next to a bucket of bones and a roll of paper towels. The third little pig eats wolf stew for supper and wears wolf-head slippers. Observant children will note that the label on Bubba's No Cook BBQ Sauce displays the face of the author-illustrator, as shown on the back flap of the book.

EXTENSION: Storytelling with Props and Music

MATERIALS

> yellow poster board
> brown poster board
> red poster board
> colored markers
> wolf puppet or mask (optional)
> tape or CD player
> musical recording of "The Three Little Pigs Blues"

PROCEDURE

The storyteller prepares three houses that the children will use to act out the story from the book or to the song "The Three Little Pigs Blues" by Greg and Steve on their recording *Greg and Steve Playing Favorites*. To make the houses, cut a window and round the top edges of the yellow straw house; add marker lines (V and W shaped) to suggest a straw appearance. Similarly, cut a window from the brown stick house, trim the top corners to make a slanted roof, and draw wiggly horizontal lines and branches to suggest twigs. Finally, for the red brick house, trim the top corners to make a slanted roof, and cut a window and attach it to the roof area to make a chimney. Draw alternating rows of rectangles to suggest bricks. (*See* figure 3.5.) Children will hold the houses up to their bodies as they peer through the windows

FIGURE 3.5 ~ Houses for *The Three Little Pigs*

wearing pink construction paper pig noses attached with masking tape or string. Another child can play the part of the wolf and use a wolf hand puppet or wear a poster board mask. Drama experiences include storytelling with props, telling stories through movement, and creative dramatics.

RECOMMENDATIONS

If using the Greg and Steve song, we divide the children who are not acting out a role into two groups. One group of children sings the wolf's line "Little pig, little pig, let me come in," and the other group sings the pigs' line "Not by the hair on my chinny chin chin." Then both groups sing together: "So he huffed and he puffed . . ." This would include antiphonal choral speaking as an additional drama experience.

ADDITIONAL EXTENSIONS

Share other versions of the traditional tale and see which rendition children like best. Some variants have been illustrated by Glen Rounds, James Marshall, Steven Kellogg, and Bruce Whatley (see

"Bibliography of Picture Books Used in Drama Extensions"). For a larger-than-life telling of *The Three Little Pigs*, enlarge the patterns that are depicted in Sierra's *Flannel Board Storytelling Book* (listed in "Drama Resource Books" at the end of this chapter). Then attach magnetic strips to the back of each piece, and, while telling the story, hang them to a blackboard, metal file cabinet, or a wall that has been painted with magnetic paint. To order magnetic paint, check Kling Magnetics: phone 800-523-9640 or e-mail info@kling.com.

Today Is Monday
Eric Carle
(Philomel)

Children can learn the days of the week while singing this popular children's song about the different food items to eat each day. Carle has chosen to depict animals eating the food, though at the end of the book, we see hungry children devouring the feast, and the animals are now just pictures hanging on the walls. This is one of the first times an illustrator depicted a child in a wheelchair in a natural setting. *Today Is Monday* was originally created as a frieze by author-illustrator Carle, who, in his picture books, makes his own paper and cuts and pastes it into a collage.

EXTENSION: Choral Speaking

MATERIALS

PROCEDURE

Divide the children into seven groups, one for each day of the week. Tell each group what day they are assigned and that they need to remember the name of the food for that particular day. Then, the storyteller reads the book, states the day of the week and pauses, with the group supplying the food name. This then becomes a cumulative choral speaking drama experience. Later, have the children sing it as a song. The music is presented in the back of Carle's book.

RECOMMENDATIONS

Children must listen very carefully for their assigned day of the week, because the days of the week are presented in reverse order. We read it quickly so that they must really pay attention, and it is much more fun. As a scaffold for the children, paste magazine cutouts of each food on cue cards. Assign a child from each group to be responsible for holding up the card each time the food item is mentioned.

ADDITIONAL EXTENSIONS

Have children write their own refrains by coming up with other foods for each day of the week and thus making a new song. Another excellent book to share for choral reading (where some children read together and then also separately) is *You Read to Me, I'll Read to You,* by Mary Ann Hoberman.

The Web Files
Margie Palatini; illustrated by Richard Egielski
(Hyperion)

Though the humor on this spoof of the former television show *Dragnet* will probably only be appreciated by adults, there is still more than enough clever wit to keep children chuckling. Ducktective Web (yes, he's a duck) and his partner, Bill, are hot on the trail of the person who has pilfered a peck of perfect purple almost-pickled peppers. The characters they interrogate are all from nursery rhymes, though the culprit turns out to be a dirty rat. Best for sophisticated children with a droll sense of humor, Egielski's illustrations are the perfect accompaniment—case closed.

EXTENSION: Charades

MATERIALS

PROCEDURE

The characters that the ducktectives interrogate are based on five nursery rhymes: "Little Miss Muffet," "Little Bo Peep," "Three Little Kittens," "Little Boy Blue," and "Little Jack Horner." (Curiously, all the characters are little.) Before presenting the story, have some children pantomime the rhymes as charades, with the other children guessing the rhyme. Tell the children who are doing the charade that they can act it out and use motions but cannot speak, except to make animal sounds. Then, when all five rhymes have been identified, share the story. Children are using pantomime and charades as drama experiences.

RECOMMENDATIONS

Have all the children sing the "Dum-De-Dum-Dum" refrain as it appears often in the story. You will need to teach them the tune, as many will not know the TV show *Dragnet.*

ADDITIONAL EXTENSION

Share another funny, urbane tale with twisted nursery rhymes playing an important role in the story. *Humpty Dumpty Egg-Splodes,* by Kevin O'Malley, is riotously funny and would also be for older children or those who have sophisticated senses of humor.

Yucka Drucka Droni
Vladimir Radunsky
(Scholastic)

Variations of this classic tongue twister can be found in Yiddish, Russian, and Danish. One of our favorites involving three sisters is in a book, now out of print, called *It's Raining, Said John Twaining,* by N. M. Bodecker. In this version, three brothers, each with an increasingly more complicated name, marry three sisters, who also each have a more difficult name than the last. The abstract, bizarre art extends this brief rhyme and creates a visual oddity that is appealing.

EXTENSION: Tongue Twisters

MATERIALS

PROCEDURE

The storyteller instructs the children to repeat each character name after she reads it. The storyteller should dramatically pause and gesture to the children so that they know to say the name. When two names are involved, the storyteller states, for example, "Yucka-Druck to Zippa Drippa," and children need to repeat that entire line. By the final marriage of the characters with the longest names, children will be faced with an extra-long tongue twister. Drama experiences include choral speaking in unison and storytelling with participation.

RECOMMENDATIONS

The book does not give text for the final, most difficult tongue twister. We add it by stating, "Yucka-Drucka-Droni to Zippa-Drippa-Limpomponi!" We have children attempt to repeat that tongue twister, and then we read the following page: "Oh, yes! That's right! Here comes the bride!"

ADDITIONAL EXTENSIONS

Have children play with additional tongue twisters. They can also make up tongue twisters based on their own names. The storyteller can also share some tongue-twister books such as *Oh Say Can You Say?* by Dr. Seuss or *Busy Buzzing Bumblebees and Other Tongue Twisters,* by Alvin Schwartz.

Bibliography of Picture Books Used in Drama Extensions

Alborough, Jez. *Duck in the Truck.* New York: HarperCollins, 1999.

Bodecker, N. M., trans. and illus. *It's Raining, Said John Twaining: Danish Nursery Rhymes.* New York: Atheneum, 1973.

Brett, Jan. *The Hat.* New York: Putnam, 1997.

_____. *The Mitten.* New York: Putnam, 1989.

Carle, Eric. *Today Is Monday.* New York: Philomel, 1993.

Christelow, Eileen. *Don't Wake Up Mama! A Five Little Monkeys Story.* New York: Clarion, 1992.

_____. *Five Little Monkeys Jumping on the Bed.* New York: Clarion, 1989.

_____. *Five Little Monkeys Sitting in a Tree.* New York: Clarion, 1991.

_____. *Five Little Monkeys Wash the Car.* Boston: Houghton Mifflin, 2000.

_____. *Five Little Monkeys with Nothing to Do.* New York: Clarion, 1996.

Climo, Shirley. *The Korean Cinderella.* Ruth Hellar, illus. New York: HarperCollins, 1993.

Day, Jon. *Let's Make Magic.* Chris Fisher, illus. New York: Kingfisher Books, 1993.

De Paola, Tomie. *Strega Nona.* New York: Simon & Schuster, 1989.

Feiffer, Jules. *Bark, George.* New York: HarperCollins, 1999.

Fox, Mem. *Hattie and the Fox.* Patricia Mullins, illus. New York: Simon & Schuster, 1986.

Galdone, Paul. *The Little Red Hen.* New York: Clarion, 1973.

_____. *The Three Billy Goats Gruff.* New York: Clarion, 1973.

Goode, Diane. *Cinderella: The Dog and Her Little Glass Slipper.* New York: Blue Sky, 2000.

Gorbachev, Valeri. *Goldilocks and the Three Bears.* New York: North-South, 2001.

Hoberman, Mary Ann. *You Read to Me, I'll Read to You.* Michael Emberley, illus. Boston: Little, Brown, 2001.

Kellogg, Steven. *Sally Ann Thunder Ann Whirlwind Crockett*. New York: Morrow, 1995.

_____. *The Three Little Pigs*. New York: Morrow, 1997.

Kimmel, Eric A. *Anansi and the Magic Stick*. Janet Stevens, illus. New York: Holiday House, 2001.

Leyton, Lawrence. *My First Magic Book: A Life-Size Guide to Making and Performing Magic Tricks*. New York: Dorling Kindersley, 1993.

Louie, Ai-Ling. *Yeh-Shen*. Ed Young, illus. New York: Putnam, 1982.

MacDonald, Margaret Read. *Fat Cat*. Julie Paschkis, illus. Little Rock, Ark.: August House Little Folk, 2001.

Marshall, James. *The Three Little Pigs*. New York: Dial, 1989.

Martin, Rafe. *The Rough-Face Girl*. David Shannon, illus. New York: Philomel, 1992.

Meddaugh, Susan. *Cinderella's Rat*. Boston: Houghton Mifflin, 1997.

_____. *Martha Speaks*. Boston: Houghton Mifflin, 1995.

Moser, Barry. *The Three Little Pigs*. Boston: Little, Brown, 2001.

O'Malley, Kevin. *Humpty Dumpty Egg-Splodes*. New York: Walker, 2001.

Palatini, Margie. *Piggie Pie!* Howard Fine, illus. New York: Clarion, 1995.

_____. *The Web Files*. Richard Egielski, illus. New York: Hyperion, 2001.

Paxton, Tom. *Going to the Zoo*. Karen Lee Schmidt, illus. New York: Morrow, 1996.

Petach, Heidi. *Goldilocks and the Three Hares*. New York: Putnam, 1995.

Plourde, Lynn. *Pigs in the Mud in the Middle of the Rud*. John Schoenherr, illus. New York: Blue Sky, 1997.

Pomerantz, Charlotte. *The Piggy in the Puddle*. James Marshall, illus. New York: Simon & Schuster, 1974.

Radunsky, Vladimir. *Yucka Drucka Droni*. New York: Scholastic, 1998.

Rounds, Glen. *Three Billy Goats Gruff*. New York: Holiday House, 1993.

_____. *Three Little Pigs and the Big Bad Wolf*. New York: Holiday House, 1992.

San Souci, Daniel. *Cendrillon*. Brian Pinkney, illus. New York: Simon & Schuster, 1998.

Schwartz, Alvin. *Busy Buzzing Bumblebees and Other Tongue Twisters*. Paul Meisel, illus. New York: HarperCollins, 1992.

Seuss, Dr. *Oh Say Can You Say?* New York: Random House, 1979.

Shepard, Aaron. *Master Man: A Tall Tale of Nigeria*. David Wisniewski, illus. New York: HarperCollins, 2001.

Steptoe, John. *Mufaro's Beautiful Daughters*. New York: Lothrop, Lee & Shepard, 1987.

Stevens, Janet, and Susan Stevens Crummel. *Cook-a-Doodle-Doo!* San Diego, Calif.: Harcourt Brace, 1999.

Sturges, Philemon. *The Little Red Hen (Makes a Pizza)*. Amy Walrod, illus. New York: Dutton, 1999.

Wattenberg, Jane. *Henny Penny*. New York: Scholastic, 2000.

Whatley, Bruce. *Wait! No Paint!* New York: HarperCollins, 2001.

Wood, Audrey. *The Bunyans*. David Shannon, illus. New York: Scholastic, 1996.

Bibliography of Musical Recordings and Videos Used in Drama Extensions

Burton, Stephanie K. *Music Mania*. Manitou Springs, Colo.: Panda Bear, 1994. (Available from Music in Motion at 800-445-0649 and <http://www.music motion.com>.)

Disney, Walt. *Walt Disney's Masterpiece Fantasia*. Burbank, Calif.: Buena Vista Home Video, 2000.

Five Little Monkeys. Long Branch, N.J.: Kimbo, 1999.

Four Baby Bumblebees. Long Branch, N.J.: Kimbo, 2001.

Greg and Steve. *Greg and Steve Playing Favorites*. Cypress, Calif.: Youngheart Music, 1991.

_____. *Greg and Steve Rockin' Down the Road*. Cypress, Calif.: Youngheart Music, 1995.

Paxton, Tom. *The Marvelous Toy*. East Hampton, N.Y.: Pax Records, 1991.

Peter, Paul, and Mary. *Peter, Paul, and Mommy*. Burbank, Calif.: Warner Brothers, 1990.

Wilson, Dean. *A Child at Heart: Songs for Children Ages 4–10*. (For ordering information, contact Dean Wilson, 466 Gardenwood Drive, Youngstown, OH 44512.)

Drama Resource Books

Barchers, Suzanne I. *Multicultural Folktales: Readers Theater for Elementary Students*. Englewood, Colo.: Teacher Ideas, 2000.

Bauer, Caroline Feller. *Presenting Reader's Theater: Plays and Poems to Read Aloud*. New York: H. W. Wilson, 1987.

Champlin, Connie. *Storytelling with Puppets*. 2d ed. Chicago: American Library Assn., 1998.

Davidson, Jane. *Emergent Literacy and Dramatic Play in Early Education*. Albany, N.Y.: Delmar, 1996.

Hunt, Tamara, and Nancy Renfro. *Puppetry in Early Childhood Education*. Austin, Tex.: Nancy Renfro Studios, 1982.

Isbell, Rebecca, and Shirley C. Raines. *Tell It Again! Easy-to-Tell Stories*. Joan C. Waites, illus. Beltsville, Md.: Gryphon House, 2000.

MacDonald, Margaret Read. *The Storyteller's Start-Up Book*. Little Rock, Ark.: August House Little Folk, 1993.

McCaslin, Nellie. *Creative Drama in the Primary Grades*. Studio City, Calif.: Players, 1987.

Raines, Shirley C., and Rebecca Isbell. *Tell It Again! 2: More Easy-to-Tell Stories*. Joan C. Waites, illus. Beltsville, Md.: Gryphon House, 2000.

Shepard, Aaron. *Stories on Stage*. New York: H. W. Wilson, 1993.

Sierra, Judy. *Flannel Board Storytelling Book*. New York: H. W. Wilson, 1987.

Stewig, John Warren, and Mary Jett-Simpson. *Language Arts in the Early Childhood Classroom*. Belmont, Calif.: Wadsworth, 1995.

Chapter Four

Extending Picture Books through Music

Music is a way of life. Children are musically inclined and perform music from infancy. When a baby coos and babbles, musical sounds are made. Even when crying, an infant varies pitch and rhythm and controls dynamics. When a parent wants to soothe the child, music is sung. Lullabies are meant to relax a baby, and rattles are a first musical instrument.

Children can use their entire bodies to make musical sounds. A mouth can sing or whistle, hands can clap or slap knees, fingers can snap, arms can wave or sway, hips shake, legs dance, feet stamp, and toes tap. We are musical creatures!

All through life, music plays a major role. It is impossible for people to get through a day without hearing music or rhythm. Musical experiences are included in all joyful happenings in our lives. Can you imagine a wedding without music? Graduation day? When we celebrate holidays, we sing or play music. And at sad times, we use music to console ourselves. Music is a vital part of our lives.

BENEFITS OF USING MUSIC WITH CHILDREN

The benefits of using music with young children are many. The following is just a partial list of some advantages derived from sharing music with youngsters.

Music, like literature, helps children understand other people, their cultures, and their ways of life.

Music helps children with their social and emotional development.

Music helps children develop their aesthetic senses.

Music provides rich language development and acquisition.

Listening skills are increased through music.

Music helps children develop self-esteem.

Music allows children to respond creatively.

Music increases children's imagination.

Children learn musical concepts of rhythm, pitch, dynamics, and timbre.

Music enhances all areas of the curriculum—it helps with sequencing when reading and with understanding concepts of sound in science, time in math, and dance in physical education.

Musical experiences foster musical appreciation.

ROLE OF ADULTS IN CHILDREN'S MUSICAL EXPERIENCES

Just as studies have shown the importance of parents as reading models to children and the impact parents have had on children's subsequent success in reading, the same has often been stated in regard to the home musical environment and the influence on children's own musicality.

Often parents and early childhood educators worry about their own musical abilities and feel they need special talent or training to use music with children. Others worry about their singing voices and fear being responsible for teaching children to sing off-key or lose pitch. Even if adults sing off-key, however, there is no lasting ill-effect on children, and they will be able to sing along in tune. Children are not music critics; rather, they respond enthusiastically to any and all attempts by teachers and librarians to use music with them. Teachers no more need to be experts in music than they do in art, math, or science to help children explore the wonders and joys of music.

It takes an adult to guide children to explore rhythm and sound. What types of musical experiences should adults provide for children? Adults should help children learn to sing in tune, show them ways to respond to rhythm through movement and personal expression, teach them to play simple instruments, and help them develop musical listening skills.

CONSIDERATIONS WHEN CHOOSING MUSIC FOR CHILDREN TO SING

Young children, preschool age through grade three (the focus of *Picture Books Plus*), are at a period of their lives when they are most actively engaged in music-making activities and are most ready to explore musical concepts. Adults should allow and encourage this open experimentation but do need to keep certain considerations in mind when selecting music for young children.

Make sure musical pieces are short.

Songs must be in the singing range of young children. Early elementary children can sing several notes higher than preschoolers, but, in general, use the eight-note rule: choose songs that run an octave, eight notes, from middle C to high C. If songs are too high or too low, children are forced to sing out of tune or will strain their voices, which can be detrimental to their vocal cords.

Songs should have small intervals (skips of the scale) between the notes. Large intervals are too difficult for young children to sing.

Pieces selected should have repetition of some sort, most often through the use of refrains.

Songs should be easy to sing, and words should be predictable and easy to remember.

Subject matter of songs should be relevant to young children's lives. (Just like selecting books, there should be no gender bias, stereotyping, etc.)

BEST WAYS TO TEACH SONGS

When using music with children, start with a song they know well. Consider this the warm-up piece. Next, teach children a new song. Finally, follow with a review of a song that you recently taught them. With young children, three songs at a time are probably sufficient.

How should you teach a new song? Even music educators disagree on this. Sue has directed a children's choir (preschool through grade two) for fifteen years, and the following is the most successful method for her. After warming up, as described above, she introduces the new song by singing it herself, so children can hear the complete song. If there is a musical tape to accompany the song, it is *not* used at this time. (The music may be too fast for children just learning a song, or the accompaniment might make it difficult for children to comprehend the words.) Then, the song is taught to the children, small section by small section, *not* line by line per se but, rather, two or three phrases at a time. Most songs have natural breaking places that complete thoughts. Teaching line by line causes a loss of continuity, and children may lose the meaning of the words. However, if children are having difficulty learning a line, you can then teach that individual line and have children echo you several times.

Just as it is important not to change unfamiliar words presented when sharing a book, the same is true for music. Instead, explain confusing words in context. And try to avoid songs with many unfamiliar words or phrasing that would make little sense to children. Granted, they may be able to learn the words by rote, but if the song makes little sense, why teach it? After the children are familiar with the song, you can add the musical tape or accompaniment.

If children are talking and not listening when you are trying to teach a new song, tell them they can use their voices during this time for singing only—not talking. If they do not wish to use their voices for singing, their voices need to remain quiet.

USING MUSICAL INSTRUMENTS WITH CHILDREN

Young children are totally fascinated by musical instruments. Experimenting with musical instruments is a very worthwhile learning experience. Children learn how a certain instrument is played and recognize the sound it makes. Also, children can apply math concepts when learning rhythm, and they feel accomplishment and pride when performing.

The most common instruments for children to play are rhythm instruments. They should be well made and have an excellent tonal quality. Avoid toy instruments at all costs. When buying instruments, purchase in sets, if possible, as it is more economical. Music in Motion (*see* "Recommended Musical Catalogs" below) has several reasonably priced sets. We recommend that if you buy a set of instruments, if finances permit, also

purchase a few extra larger drums and tambourines (these are popular instruments, and larger drums are not often included in sets). Sets normally include triangles, wrist bells, ankle bells, claves, rhythm sticks, small tambourines, a small drum, and sand blocks. Make sure you have enough instruments for the number of children you have; if not, allow every child a chance to play some instrument by him- or herself.

Some simple musical instruments can be made (*see* "Extension: Making Musical Instruments" below). However, homemade instruments (a wonderful teaching tool for children to understand how sounds are made) should not replace real musical instruments.

If you have access to a guitar, an Autoharp, or a small keyboard or piano, show children (briefly, depending on age) how to play it, and allow all children a chance to play a few notes. Sue has found that even young children will eagerly wait in line for their turns and that they understand they only get a few tries before the next child in line takes a turn. Children are fascinated by the sound of these larger instruments and are thrilled that they are able to "play" them.

PROFESSIONAL APPROACHES TO TEACHING MUSIC TO YOUNG CHILDREN

There are four main methodologies for teaching music education—the Dalcroze Method, the Koda'ly Method, the Orff Method, and the Suzuki Method. Most educators employ one of these methods when teaching music to young children. Choose one or a combination as meets your programming needs.

Swiss composer Emile Jaques-Dalcroze believed that rhythm was the fundamental force in music. His approach, in fact, is often called Eurhythmics (meaning rhythmic movement). Dalcroze felt that children should learn first by the use of rhythmic body movement and then by ear training and that instrumental study should not be introduced until after children mastered those skills.

Zoltán Koda'ly was a Hungarian composer and a firm believer that children learn music by making their own music and that the first and most important instrument is the child's own voice. Instruction in singing should begin in the early years, and the piano is considered a negative diversion. Instead, Koda'ly recommended that children's percussion and barred instruments be used to accompany their songs. Play songs, games, and chants are important for the teaching of rhythm.

Carl Orff, a German composer and music educator, believed that music, speech, and movement should be combined when teaching music. Probably most famous for his specially designed percussion and keyboard instruments, Orff felt that instruments should be played from memory and that serious musical lessons with drills came only after other musical skills were learned. His perfectly pitched instruments—xylophones, metallophones, and glockenspiels—are rather expensive but quite popular.

Shinichi Suzuki was a Japanese violinist who believed that children must first develop an ear for music rather than learn to read notes. His method of teaching even very young children (three- and four-year-olds) how to play classical music on their miniature violins is controversial to some. Parental involvement is key to this approach, and parents must attend weekly lessons and supervise their children's practice.

COMMON MUSICAL TERMS THAT CAN BE TAUGHT TO CHILDREN

Just as literature has its own language to learn and understand (plot, characters, voice, etc.), the language of music should be taught. Children readily understand and quickly apply these terms to their own musical activities.

Beat—The pulse that can be heard or felt in music

Dynamics—The various degrees of sound, such as loud or soft, used to create a mood or make a point

Harmony—Two or more tones sounded simultaneously

Melody—The succession of musical tones moving up or down that forms one aspect of a musical piece

Pitch—The highness or lowness of a tone

Rhythm—Regularly occurring beats of different lengths or stresses forming the pattern of the piece of music. This is the first musical concept children learn.

Tempo—The actual speed of the music

Timbre—Refers to the tonal quality of the sound, whether it be the voice or an instrument

MUSICAL EXPERIENCES USED IN OUR EXTENSIONS

The following musical experiences can successfully be used with young children and are beneficial for musical instruction (and fun!). The musical extensions in this chapter incorporate all of these methods of musical expression.

Singing or learning to sing

Learning rhythm or beat

Chanting

Rapping

Acting out a song

Developing language

Using recorded music

Playing instruments

Making instruments

Moving or marching to music

Making up new songs

Listening to music

Playing musical games

Call and response, or echoing

Learning a refrain

Employing a twisted song

Appreciating contemporary music

Composing lyrics

RECOMMENDED MUSICAL CATALOGS

In our extensions in this chapter (and in other chapters), we refer often to several companies, particularly Music in Motion. This company's catalog has a wealth of musical instruments, rhythm sticks, rainbow wands, scarves for musical movement, song picture books, and more. The quality of the products is superb, and we highly recommend this company. Their telephone number is 800-445-0649, and the web site is <http://www.musicmotion.com>.

Our most common source for musical tapes or CDs is a company called New Sound, where both libraries and schools can receive a substantial discount, and customer service is very helpful (particularly if you want to know if a recording is still available). Contact New Sound at 800-342-0295 or <http://www.allegro-music.com>.

We also use Kimbo and Educational Record Center (though New Sound gives a larger discount to educational institutions than these individual companies). Contact Kimbo at 800-631-2187 or <http://www.kimboed.com>; contact Educational Record Center at 888-372-4543 or <http://www.erckids.com>.

Get ready to sway your body, tap your toes, and clap your hands. We promise that our musical activities will bring some joy to your day and will lighten your spirit!

MUSIC EXTENSIONS

Bein' with You This Way
W. Nikola-Lisa; illustrated by Michael Bryant
(Lee & Low)

Children from various ethnic backgrounds are depicted playing games in a city park and also using playground equipment. The accompanying text is a playground rap, discussing the children's physical differences and pointing out that even with these differences, the children have many similarities. Bright oranges, greens, reds, and browns predominate in the watercolor and pencil illustrations.

EXTENSION: Rap

MATERIALS

PROCEDURE

This book has a natural beat, or rhythm, to the text. Share the book first, and then share it a second time, reading it as if it were a rap. Have children join in by snapping their fingers and tapping their toes as suggested at the beginning of the story. You can also have children clap their hands, but first explain to them how to clap for this. Rather than clapping with full hands, which would be too loud for a group of children to hear the rap, tell the children to use their hands as if they are playing a musical instrument. The fingers of one hand should be clapped against the bottom of the palm of the other hand, as if they are playing a drum. Musical experiences include rapping and learning rhythm or beat.

RECOMMENDATIONS

Many younger children do not have the fully developed muscle coordination necessary to snap their fingers, so recommend they clap by "playing" their hands and tapping their toes. You can also have children use rhythm sticks. You must practice reading the book as a rap several times until you get the flow of the rhythm. Also, you will need to type the words on a sheet of paper (or have someone hold the book and turn the pages for you) so that when you share it the second time, your hands are free to snap the beat as you verbally rap the text. To keep the beat, you may need to add some extra words to a section or change the text slightly.

ADDITIONAL EXTENSION

Lead the children in a discussion of people's diverse physical characteristics including similarities and differences. Even though we may look different in size or shape or in coloring, we are all wonderful in our own way. Encourage them to express how much they enjoy being with other children or adults who are not the same as them.

Cat Goes Fiddle-I-Fee
Paul Galdone
(Houghton Mifflin)

This story is based on an old English rhyme. Author-illustrator Galdone uses a farm boy in his illustrations and shows him feeding the various animals by a tree on the farm. The repetitive cumulative text provides the perfect vehicle for children to quickly learn the words and sing along. The animals are easy to identify in Galdone's comical style of illustrations.

EXTENSION: **Clothesline Song**

MATERIALS

> clothesline
>
> clothespins
>
> poster board animal pieces

PROCEDURE

Share the book first so children can see the illustrations, but sing the text so they will know the tune of the song. Then, tie both ends of a long piece of clothesline to sturdy pillars, posts, or weighted chair backs. You can also have other adults hold the ends of the clothesline. Give each child a poster board animal or clothespins. Sing the song again, and have the child bring up the corresponding animal during that verse, and have another child attach it to the line with the clothespins. The benefit of using a clothesline with a cumulative song is that children must sing the animal sounds in reverse each time plus add an additional sound. Visually seeing the pieces on the line provides scaffolding that helps children remember the order of the animals. Musical experiences include singing and developing language.

RECOMMENDATIONS

To make poster board animals, find pattern books with copyright permission given for pattern use, and enlarge them on a copier or by using an opaque projector to project them on a wall. Attach poster board to the wall with a piece of masking tape, and trace the animal patterns. To

use a recording of this song, consult *Where Is Thumbkin?* for a version titled "Fiddle-I-Fee."

ADDITIONAL EXTENSION

Share another clothesline story or song, such as *Old MacDonald Had a Farm*. We like the version illustrated by Glen Rounds because it has a skunk for the last animal. During the "pee-yoo" refrain, you can unclip the clothespins one by one, releasing the animals so that they can escape the skunk smell.

Cows in the Kitchen
June Crebbin; illustrated by Katharine McEwen
(Candlewick)

While Tom Farmer is asleep in a haystack, the farm animals enter the house and create chaos, from cows prancing in the kitchen to pigs "pigging out" in the pantry. Finally, a dog and little white mouse wake up Tom Farmer, and he shoos all the animals out of the house. He then continues his nap in his armchair while the farm animals sneak into the house and awaken him again. Bright watercolors and pencil were used to depict the frantic farmhouse scenes.

EXTENSION: **Learning Dynamics in Music**

MATERIALS

> none

PROCEDURE

Sing the text to the tune of "Skip to My Lou." Children can sing the text the whole way through as soon as they identify the animal on the page and its location. Or, you can sing the first line of each verse, and children can join in easily, because of the repetitive lines. There are two sections of the text where the children are required to sing softly (when the farmer is sleeping in the haystack and when the animals sneak back in the house and wake up the farmer again). You can teach children the concept of dynamics—singing loudly for some parts and softly for other sections. Musical experiences include singing, developing language, and employing a twisted song (changing the words to the tune of "Skip to My Lou").

RECOMMENDATIONS

You might wish to share the illustrations in the book first *before* reading or singing the text. Ask the children to identify the animal and the sound it makes as well as the animal's location. The first four verses are alliterative.

ADDITIONAL EXTENSION

Sing Raffi's song "Down on Grandpa's Farm" on the recording *One Light, One Sun* that allows children to make many animal sounds. You can also sing "Old MacDonald Had a Farm."

Crocodile Beat
Gail Jorgensen; illustrated by Patricia Mullins
(Bradbury)

Down by the river in the heat of the day,
the crocodile sleeps and awaits his prey.

Meanwhile, the other jungle animals are playing near the riverbank, creating their own special musical jungle beat. When the crocodile awakens, he thinks he will have an easy time finding dinner until King Lion steps in, and all the crocodile gets in his jaws for dinner is Lion's red throne. Bright tissue paper collage and crayon were used in the illustrations.

EXTENSION: Learning Rhythm

MATERIALS

rhythm sticks

PROCEDURE

This story lends itself well to being read in a simple rhythmic pattern with four beats to a measure. The repeated rhythm is one measure of half note, half note and then another measure of quarter note, quarter note, half note. On most pages you simply need to repeat one more animal sound to keep the rhythmic pattern flowing. (The perfect page to feel the beat is the one with the

elephants and the sound "Boom, Boom, Boom-Boom-Boom!") Make sure you practice reading the text in the rhythmic pattern before presenting it. Next, teach the pattern to children using rhythm sticks or drums. After they have the beat, read the story again and see if they can keep the beat with you. Musical experiences include learning rhythm, chanting, developing language, and playing instruments.

RECOMMENDATION

Stop the beat after the words "Here he comes with a glint in his eye," and read the words on the last three double-page spreads emphatically.

ADDITIONAL EXTENSION

Another book to try with an identical rhythmic pattern is Nancy Van Laan's *Possum Come a-Knockin'*. For additional fun with rhythmic patterns, have children one by one try to imitate a pattern that you beat out with rhythm sticks. Give each child a different pattern to imitate. Or, you may wish to use Hap Palmer's award-winning recording *Rhythms on Parade*, which is specifically written for hand claps, rhythm sticks, and rhythm instruments.

Here Come the Aliens!
Colin McNaughton
(Candlewick)

A fleet of spaceships heads toward Earth with some pretty fearsome, smelly, multiheaded aliens on board. Their goal is to conquer the human race. Because they speak alien language (grunts, burps, and squeaks), the chance of peace talks is nil. Right before they land on Earth, a piece of paper picturing ugly Earth creatures (children) scares them off. Brightly colored aliens cavort across the star-studded, black outer-space backdrop.

EXTENSION: Cued Responses

MATERIALS

tape or CD player

musical recording of a song with non-sense words

PROCEDURE

Every fourth line of the story (except for the surprise ending) has a repeated refrain: "The aliens are coming!" Hold an alien puppet in your hand when reading this story and have the alien point to the children when they must shout out their response. Our alien puppet is from Folkmanis puppets, <http://www.folkmanis.com>, though there may be other sources. After sharing the pages in the book where the aliens are speaking their language—a mixture of grunts, burps, and squeaks—play a song with nonsense words. (Try Greg and Steve's "Scat Like That," on the recording *On the Move with Greg and Steve,* which is a call-and-response, or echo, song.) Then, have the children speak (squeak) some alien language. Musical experiences include developing language, using recorded music, and call and response, or echoing.

RECOMMENDATIONS

Near the end of the book, where the age of the children is mentioned, we substitute the words "what's more" for "aged four," which fits perfectly and makes the story suitable to tell to a mixed age group or a class of children of another age (besides age four)!

ADDITIONAL EXTENSIONS

Serve gummy worms! The aliens eating lunch are munching on what looks just like worms. Sing the song mentioned in the text, "Twinkle, Twinkle, Little Star." Then, read another story about aliens, Daniel Kirk's *Hush Little Alien.* Tell the children that the story you are going to read is written in rhyme and is about aliens and outer space. Explain that you are going to sing the story but leave off the last word of each rhyme and that the alien puppet will point to a child who must supply the missing word. Remind the children that the word must rhyme and be about aliens or objects in space. Then, *without showing them the illustrations* and holding the book so only you can see it, read the story, point your alien puppet at an unsuspecting child, and have him or her supply the missing word. You may show the illustration if the child is having trouble guessing the rhyming word.

If You're Happy and You Know It
David A. Carter
(Scholastic)

The traditional song is accompanied by illustrations of a cat clapping her hands, a dog wagging his tail, a skunk patting her head, a chicken flapping her wings, an owl winking his eyes, and a mouse touching his toes. For each creature, there is a pull-tab with the animal performing the motion described. At the end, a huge pop-up has all the characters shouting "Hooray!"

EXTENSION: **Extending a Traditional Song**

MATERIALS

tape or CD player

musical recording of "If You're Happy and You Know It"

PROCEDURE

Play a version of "If You're Happy and You Know It" and have the children sing along and perform the actions. We like Greg and Steve's version on the recording *We All Live Together, Volume 3.* Another good version that follows the text of the book can be found on *Kindergarten Hits,* recorded by Kidzup. After several repetitions of the song, ask the children what other movements they could make to convey happiness, for example, "slap their knees" or "jump for joy." Sing the song again, and this time extend the traditional piece with the children's added verses. Note that the animals in the story are all wearing clothing. Sing the song again and have the children wear dress-up clothing and then add motions for the animals to do with their clothing, such as "pull your collar" or "flap your apron" or "raise your hat." Musical experiences include singing, developing language, acting out a song, composing lyrics, and using recorded music.

RECOMMENDATIONS

Let the children be creative about their suggestions of movements. If they mention something lengthy, add extra notes to the song to accommodate their suggestion. If they give incorrect grammar, correct it. If you have a small group of children, let each child mention a movement. With a large group, take as many suggestions as you have time for, and when you run out of time, let the children share their ideas with their neighbors.

ADDITIONAL EXTENSIONS

Discuss with children what other emotions they feel besides happiness and how they can change the song to include these other feelings. For example, "If you're angry and you know it, stamp your feet." Then, discuss with children how they handle their emotions. When they are angry, what do they do to "cool down"? Share Molly Bang's *When Sophie Gets Angry—Really, Really Angry . . .* to discover how Sophie handled her anger. Children can make a book and draw pictures of themselves and what they are doing when they are happy, sad, angry, and so forth. On the same Greg and Steve recording *(We All Live Together, Volume 3),* the selection "Sing a Happy Song" fits nicely as a follow-up to this activity.

Little White Duck
Walt Whippo;
music by Bernard Zaritzky;
illustrated by Joan Paley
(Little, Brown)

A popular children's song is illustrated to appear as a stage presentation, with a mouse narrator, and featuring the main characters of the little white duck, the little green frog, the little black bug, and the little red snake. The bright collages are a combination of cut paper, watercolor, crayon, and pastel. Textured and colored papers were cut and layered to create a three-dimensional effect. The music for the song is included in the front of the book along with guitar or Autoharp chords.

EXTENSION: **Musical Play**

MATERIALS

> table
> poster board cutouts of characters
> colored markers
> paint stirrers
> blue sheets or blue poster board
> green poster board

PROCEDURE

The librarian or teacher or the children can make a poster board cutout for each of the characters in the book. Patterns can be copied from a pattern book with copyright permission given for pattern use and enlarged on a copier or by using an overhead or opaque projector to project them on a wall. Attach poster board to the wall with a piece of masking tape, and trace the animal patterns. Using brightly colored poster board allows children to complete the characters by simply adding features with colored markers. Cut out the characters and glue or tape them to the paint stirrers. Using a table for a stage, place a blue sheet or blue poster board over the front of the table to give the appearance of the water. Also, add a green poster board lily pad to the blue sheet for the setting. Children can then act out the play as given in the book. Musical experiences include acting out a song and singing.

RECOMMENDATIONS

For more effect, hang a blue sheet or blue poster board as a backdrop on the wall for the sky. We recommend that you make double-sided stick puppets to allow each character to reverse its direction. Some of the children can use the stick puppets while other children stand by the side of the table and sing the song (as an accompanying choir).

ADDITIONAL EXTENSION

A nice recording of "Little White Duck" can be found on *Six Little Ducks.* Have the children learn the song by singing it several times through before acting out the play. Sing other duck songs such as "Six Little Ducks," which can also be found on the recording *Six Little Ducks,* or "Five Little Ducks," recorded on *Where Is Thumbkin?*

My Favorite Things
Richard Rodgers and Oscar Hammerstein II;
illustrated by Renee Graef
(HarperCollins)

One of the most popular songs from Rodgers and Hammerstein's musical *The Sound of Music* is lavishly illustrated with bordered double-page spreads. In this book, a mother and two of her children describe their favorite things. The musical score with full accompaniment is included after the text.

EXTENSION: Singing to Recorded Music

MATERIALS

> tape or CD player
>
> musical recording of "My Favorite Things"

PROCEDURE

Play a recording of "My Favorite Things" from the film version of the Broadway musical *The Sound of Music.* You can turn the pages of the book and show the pictures while the song is being played. Then, have the children join in singing along with the recording. Later, have the children share what some of their favorite things are for each season of the year. Musical experiences include singing to recorded music and appreciating contemporary music.

RECOMMENDATIONS

On the recording, Julie Andrews speaks some of the words rather than singing them. Children can sing over the spoken words. You may need to practice the song with them several times until they learn it. The musical accompaniment is included at the back of the book with guitar or Autoharp chords added. If you or someone else can play the music, have the children sing along to the live music for a different experience.

ADDITIONAL EXTENSION

On the same recording, play the song "Do-Re-Mi." This song is a musical explanation of the notes of a musical scale, which children can readily learn by singing this song. Motions can also easily accompany this song. Another way to learn the scale is by using the animals crab (c), donkey (d), elephant (e), fish (f), gorilla (g), alligator (a), and beaver (b) on a musical staff, as offered in the Music in Motion catalog. (For ordering information, *see* "Recommended Musical Catalogs" above.)

Old Black Fly
Jim Aylesworth; illustrated by Stephen Gammell
(Henry Holt)

An old black fly creates chaos in a household that is about to celebrate a birthday with an elaborate chocolate cake covered by pink frosting. Every verse of the rhymed text ends with the refrain "Shoo fly! Shoo fly! Shooo." The mischief the fly creates occurs in an alphabetical sequence. The birthday cake finally ends the life of the pesky fly, and the last blue page makes it appear that the fly has gone off to "fly heaven." Black endpapers, representing the fly, establish the mood at the beginning of the book. Paint splatters by the creative artist, Gammell, show the progression of the fly's movements.

EXTENSION: Singing a Refrain

MATERIALS

> fly puppet or flyswatter

PROCEDURE

The entire text of this song can be sung to a variation of the traditional American spiritual "Joshua Fit the Battle of Jericho" with some musical and word adjustments. Beginning on the first left-hand page of the text, repeat the words "apple pie" three times just as you have done on the first page for "buzzin' around." This is true for the repetition of the last three syllables on every left-hand page of the book. First, teach the children how to sing "Shoo fly! Shoo fly! Shooo" to the notes for the words "walls came tumbling down," or the musical notes, G, F, E, D, C. (*See* figure 4.1.) Every time this line recurs, point to the children with a flyswatter or fly puppet so they know to sing the refrain. Once you have practiced this, you can then begin the story and sing it the whole way through. Musical experiences include singing, learning rhythm or beat, and learning a refrain.

Shoo fly! Shoo fly! Shooo.

FIGURE 4.1 ~ Music for *Old Black Fly*

RECOMMENDATIONS

When you finish this alphabet book, with the letter Z, you can swat the flyswatter down hard, or "swat" the book closed, and then reopen it to show the double-spread "swat" page. This creates a surprise element for the children. When singing the text, sing the last few lines slowly, for effect. At the end of the story, ask the children what created the swat. Most children will respond, "A flyswatter!" even if you are not using the flyswatter as a prop. Then, show them that it was not a flyswatter but, rather, the cake. Point out that the colors on the "swat" page match the colors of the cake.

ADDITIONAL EXTENSIONS

A wonderful story to share after *Old Black Fly* is *You Can't Catch Me,* by Joanne Oppenheim. This is a takeoff on *The Gingerbread Boy* with a repeated refrain of "'No matter how hard you try, try, try, you can't catch me,' called the pesky black fly." Children can join in with this refrain also. Or, for a third choice, use a version of *I Know an Old Lady Who Swallowed a Fly* that also employs a repeated refrain. For another fly song, sing the version of "Skip to My Lou" on Pamela Conn Beall and Susan Hagen Nipp's recording *Wee Sing and Play.*

Papa, Please Get the Moon for Me
Eric Carle
(Simon & Schuster)

Monica asks Papa to get the Moon from the sky for her. Papa takes a very long ladder and places it on top of a very high mountain so that he can reach the Moon. When it gets smaller and is just the right size, Papa takes it to his daughter, who plays with it as it gets smaller and smaller and finally disappears. It finally reappears back in the sky to Monica's delight. Carle's famous tissue-paper collage is used for the illustrations, and, in addition, several pages fold out to display very large pictures.

EXTENSION: Playing Instruments on Cue

MATERIALS

> rhythm sticks
>
> maracas
>
> tambourines
>
> lollipop drums or other drums
>
> a soup ladle

PROCEDURE

A perfect song to sing after sharing this story is "Aiken Drum." One version of this song can be found on Raffi's *Singable Songs for the Very Young.* Sing through the song first so that children know it and will be able to sing along later when you use musical instruments. Then, pick some children to play instruments, and have the rest of the children sing. Perform the song several times so that all the children have a chance to play instruments. Recommended instruments for this song are maracas, rhythm sticks, tambourines, and lollipop (or other) drums. (Lollipop drums and other instruments are available from Music in Motion; *see* "Recommended Musical Catalogs" above.) We recommend these instruments because they are not as loud as others are, and the children will still be able to hear the singing. Assign the instruments to children, and have one child use a rhythm stick to strike against a soup ladle in time to the music. Instruct the children as follows: for each verse that has "And he played upon a ladle," only the child with the soup ladle should accompany the singing by keeping the beat. For all other verses, the other children play and keep the beat, but not the child with the ladle. The ladle verse repeats several times. By performing the piece this way, children use listening skills to know which verse they should play and which verse they should not play. Musical experiences include learning to sing, learning rhythm or beat, playing instruments, and listening to music.

RECOMMENDATIONS

It is particularly helpful for younger children if the librarian or teacher directs the playing of instruments by pointing to the child (or children) who is to be playing with one hand and holding up the other hand with a "stop" motion so that that child (or children) knows not to play. Though directing is very useful, children still need to pay attention and listen for their part.

ADDITIONAL EXTENSION

Because the song and story are both about the Moon, some simple science concepts can be explained. Ask the children if the Moon actually gets larger and smaller as mentioned in the story. (No—the Moon only appears to change size, waxing and waning, because of the way the sun reflects on the moon and our varying view of it, based on both bodies' rotations.)

Saturday Night at the Dinosaur Stomp
Carol Diggory Shields;
illustrated by Scott Nash
(Candlewick)

The word goes out during prehistoric time that all dinosaurs are invited to Saturday night's dinosaur stomp. So all the dinosaurs scrub their necks and nails, brush their teeth, and curl their tails, and the dance begins! From the Triassic Twist to the Brontosaurus Bump, to the Raptor Rap and Jurassic Jump, there never was a party like the Dinosaur Stomp! Illustrations were rendered in bright watercolors and pencil.

EXTENSION: Dancing to Music

MATERIALS

> tape or CD player
> musical recording of "Dinosaur Rock 'N' Roll"

PROCEDURE

The endpapers of this book delineate several dinosaur dances with easy-to-learn steps. Have children learn one or two of the dances, and then play a song about dinosaurs that has a lively beat. A perfect example is "Dinosaur Rock 'N' Roll," by Joanie Bartels, on the recording *Dancin' Magic*. Children can perform the steps given in the book or make up their own dinosaur dance. We have provided two modified versions of dances shown in the endpapers that we think children should easily be able to imitate. For example, to do the "Supersaurus Circle Stomp" (as shown in figure 4.2), each child chooses a spot on the floor where his or her body can move around in a circle. One foot stays in the center, pivoting, while the other foot "stomps" in a circle around the center foot and points in a new direction with each step of the stomp. The "Stegosaurus Square Stomp" can be done by placing squares on the floor and moving clockwise around the square, as shown in figure 4.2. Start in the lower right corner with the right foot; step to the left with both feet, using the left foot first. Step forward with the left foot and to the side with both feet, right foot first. Musical

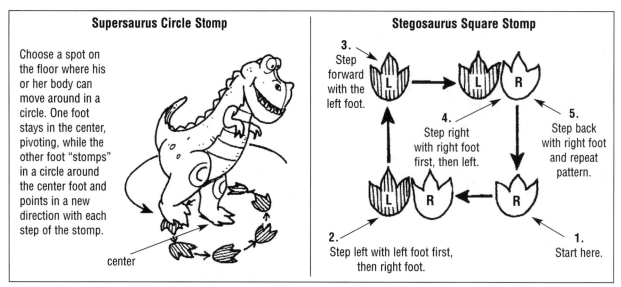

FIGURE 4.2 ~ Dances for *Saturday Night at the Dinosaur Stomp*

experiences include dancing to music, learning a beat, and listening to music.

RECOMMENDATIONS

The reader should practice the dinosaur names several times before presenting the book orally. Unfortunately, the book does not provide the phonetic pronunciation of the many difficult dinosaur names, so it may be necessary to consult a reference book or the Internet. The book also mentions a *brontosaurus,* which we now know really did not exist. (Scientists attached the wrong head to a dinosaur body and called it a *brontosaurus.* When they realized their mistake, they renamed the corrected version an *apatosaurus.*) Also, the song "Dinosaur Rock 'N' Roll" mentions that dinosaurs danced to a caveman band, so you may want to point out that cavemen did not exist during the dinosaurs' era.

ADDITIONAL EXTENSIONS

Another excellent recording with several dinosaur songs is Jane Murphy and Dennis Buck's *Once upon a Dinosaur.* Two songs we particularly like are "Fossil Rock" and "Dinosaur Dance." "Fossil Rock," which describes the years of hard work and study by paleontologists that allow us to know so much about dinosaurs, has a repetitious refrain that children can sing. "Dinosaur Dance" describes several different types of dinosaurs and is another good song to use when performing dance steps from the book. For older children, share an outstanding book about Waterhouse Hawkins, the first gentleman to painstakingly assemble dinosaur bones, so that today we know what dinosaurs looked like. The book is titled *The Dinosaurs of Waterhouse Hawkins,* by Barbara Kerley.

The Seals on the Bus
Lenny Hort
(Henry Holt)

This twisted version of the popular song "The Wheels on the Bus" has seals, tigers, geese, rabbits, monkeys, vipers, sheep, and skunks making their own special sounds and actions. When the skunks spray, all the people on the bus scream for help, but, fortunately, they can disembark because they have arrived at their destination—a big party! Cut paper, gouache, acrylics, and pencils were used to create the illustrations.

EXTENSION: Twisted Song

MATERIALS

PROCEDURE

This story is a twisted version of "The Wheels on the Bus," so many children may be familiar with the tune. On the first reading, have the children join in on the animal sounds or movements. Next, assign the children the role of an animal that appears in the story—seals, tigers, geese, rabbits, monkeys, vipers, sheep, and skunks—and people. Have them listen for their part and make the appropriate sound or movement. Discuss where they think the animals are heading on the bus. Have the children make up their own verses for this song by choosing different animals. Musical experiences include employing a twisted song, developing language, and making up songs.

RECOMMENDATIONS

Allow the children to choose their parts. Say, for example, "I need five seals. Who wants to be a seal?" Allowing the children to make nonthreatening decisions now helps them later when they must make more important decisions. For older children, challenge them to choose animals from a given habitat, for example, the woodlands, a jungle, or a polar region.

ADDITIONAL EXTENSIONS

The animals in this story are all commonly found in a zoo. Share another song about the zoo and its animals such as "Going to the Zoo" (chapter 3 describes ways to act out this storybook and song). Another extension is to compare different storybook versions of this song such as Raffi's *Wheels on the Bus* or Paul O. Zelinsky's *The Wheels on the Bus*.

She'll Be Comin' Round the Mountain
adapted by Tom Birdseye and
Debbie Holsclaw Birdseye;
illustrated by Andrew Glass
(Holiday House)

Oma and Opa Sweet and the entire Sweet clan tell the young twins, Petunia and Delbert, about their dear friend Tootie, who is planning to come around the mountain and visit. Tootie, who wears slop boots and jeans and brings along her farm critters in her old jalopy, always dances a little jig, throws back her head, and screams "Yahoo!" So, when the finely dressed lady wearing silk gloves arrives in a new car, the Sweet clan is not even sure if she is Tootie, until she throws back her head and yodels "Yahoo!" Twisted verses are added to the traditional Appalachian song, and music and chords are included at the back of the book.

EXTENSION: **Participation Song and Twisted Versions**

MATERIALS

> tape or CD player
>
> musical recording of "She'll Be Comin' 'Round the Mountain"
>
> musical recording of a twisted version of "She'll Be Comin' Round the Mountain"

PROCEDURE

First, sing the traditional version of "She'll Be Comin' 'Round the Mountain" on the recording of Pamela Conn Beall and Susan Hagen Nipp's *Wee Sing*. Then, read the Birdseyes' twisted version, and have the children participate by singing the interjections that are shown in parentheses, such as "Yes, indeed!" "Mighty fine!" and "Swish! Swish!" Finally, share the twisted song version that is recorded on Greg and Steve's *We All Live Together, Volume 2*, titled "She'll Be Coming 'Round the Mountain." Musical experiences include singing, listening to recorded music, learning a refrain, and using a twisted song.

RECOMMENDATIONS

Read the story with a hillbilly accent. If possible, accompany the song with an Autoharp or guitar, using the music included in the back of the book, as it is easy to play. Explain how one plays an Autoharp (or guitar), and let the children have a chance to strum a chord.

ADDITIONAL EXTENSION

Make and play kitchen instruments! Examples are tapping two spoons together, strumming a grater or heating vent with a butter knife, turning the handle of a grinder or Foley food mill, rapping a spoon on a metal colander, playing a kazoo made from a comb covered on both sides with wax paper and humming against it, and clanging two pan lids.

Summertime
George Gershwin, DuBose Heyward,
Dorothy Heyward, and Ira Gershwin;
illustrated by Mike Wimmer
(Simon & Schuster)

Probably the most well known song from the *Porgy and Bess* folk opera, *Summertime* features illustrator Wimmer depicting an African American family from the last century enjoying summertime activities. The dramatic and glorious oil paintings rendered on canvas are beautiful works of art. A musical score is included.

EXTENSION: **Adding Motions and Movement to a Song**

MATERIALS

 tape or CD player

 musical recording of "Summertime" from *Porgy and Bess*

 rainbow scarves

 rainbow ribbon wands

PROCEDURE

If you feel comfortable doing so, sing the words of the story the first time through, allowing the children to appreciate the beautiful artwork. On the second singing, add motions to go along with the words, such as swinging on a rope, pretending to fish, picking cotton, rocking a baby. Then, play the piece from the American opera. Children can use movement and musical interpretation with the rainbow scarves or rainbow ribbon wands or both. These are available for purchase from Music in Motion (*see* "Recommended Musical Catalogs"

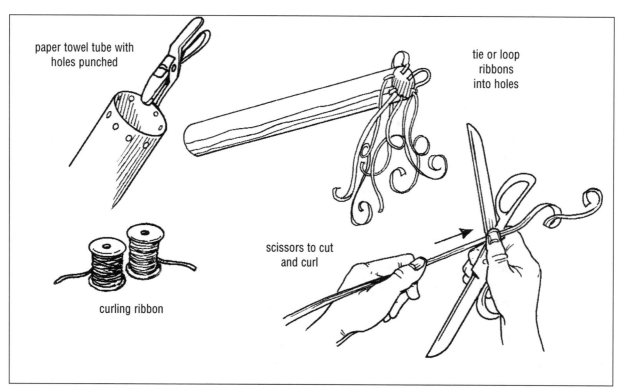

paper towel tube with holes punched

tie or loop ribbons into holes

scissors to cut and curl

curling ribbon

FIGURE 4.3 ～ Rainbow Ribbon Wand for *Summertime*

above). Musical experiences include using recorded music, listening to music, appreciating classical music, and moving and dancing to music.

RECOMMENDATIONS

If there are financial considerations, use real scarves instead. Older children can make their own rainbow ribbon wands by attaching brightly colored curlable wrapping ribbons to an empty paper towel roll (or dowel) and curling the ends of the ribbons as shown in figure 4.3. To create a summertime atmosphere, use a heat lamp, cautioning children to avoid touching the bulb or hot metal.

ADDITIONAL EXTENSION

Have the children share their favorite summertime activities. Younger children can act out their favorite activities; older children can pantomime their favorites and have other children guess what the activity is. Serve lemonade or snow cones.

Teddy Bears' Picnic
Jerry Garcia and David Grisman;
illustrated by Bruce Whatley
(HarperCollins)

Words from the popular children's song are accompanied by illustrations of teddy bears carrying food (and musical instruments) to their picnic in the woods. Whatley's fun-loving bears are very child appealing. Brown, tan, and green colors predominate in the illustrations. Though no musical arrangement is included in the text, a cassette tape is included with the book.

EXTENSION: **Parachute Play**

MATERIALS

parachute (or king-sized fitted sheet)

PROCEDURE

After reading the story, play the tape that accompanies this book. Children can pretend they are teddy bears. Begin with the "bears" marching to their picnic site where the parachute is laying. Then, using the parachute, create a hideaway picnic area with children crawling under the parachute. A more exciting way to play this is to have the children march around in a circle holding on to the handles of the parachute (or the sides of the sheet). When they want to hide, they should all throw their hands up in the air while still holding on to the handles, and then pull the parachute down as they step forward, letting it mushroom overhead and then slowly descend as it envelops them. (*See* figure 4.4.) Musical experiences

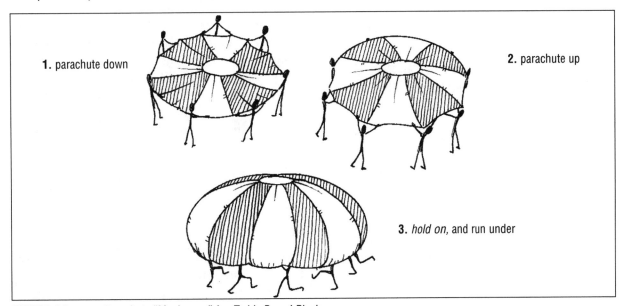

1. parachute down

2. parachute up

3. *hold on,* and run under

FIGURE 4.4 ~ Parachute "Mushroom" for *Teddy Bears' Picnic*

include moving and marching to music and playing a musical game.

RECOMMENDATIONS

A parachute can be purchased from Music in Motion (*see* "Recommended Musical Catalogs" above) or a king-sized fitted sheet can be substituted. There are several other illustrated picture book versions of this song that we prefer, but they were out of print as we were writing this book. A newer board book version of this book, written by Jimmy Kennedy and illustrated by Michael Hague, is also available.

ADDITIONAL EXTENSION

Hold a teddy bear picnic! Children may bring their bears with them on Teddy Bear Day. (Provide extras for bearless children.) Have children lay their bears on top of the parachute, pick the parachute up, and do the "wave" by alternating their arms up in the air and pulling them down again quickly. The bears will bounce around on the parachute. Spread out a blanket and serve treats. Children can introduce their "friend." Sing other teddy bear songs. An energetic recording with numerous teddy bear songs (including another version of "Teddy Bears' Picnic") can be found on *Teddy Bears' Picnic,* by Gary Rosen.

Thump, Thump, Rat-a-Tat-Tat
Gene Baer; illustrated by Lois Ehlert
(HarperCollins)

A marching band is coming to town. The text font is small and the band is soft when it is far away. As the band gets closer, the text gets larger and the band grows louder. The repetition of "thump, thump" and "rat-a-tat-tat" gives the text a musical quality. Ehlert combines graphical shapes to depict the musicians, drum majors, flags, trumpets, trombones, tubas, flutes, side drums, and bass drums.

EXTENSION: Marching in a Parade

MATERIALS

PROCEDURE

Everyone gets to participate in this marching parade! First, read the story and teach the concept of dynamics. Tell the children to think of a parade coming to town and how it would sound if it were far away in the distance. Then, ask them how it would sound when it reached them and how soft it would become as it left town. This will help them understand the concept of dynamics—starting softly, getting louder, and then becoming softer again. You might also point out to older children how the musicians in the book get larger and smaller and how the font also becomes larger and smaller as the parade enters and leaves town. Then, divide the children into two groups. Have one group of children say, "Rat-a-tat-tat" and the other group say, "Thump, thump." After they have practiced, tell them that they are in a parade, and because it is far away at first, they need to start softly, gradually get louder, and eventually become softer again. The storyteller will read every line *except* for the "rat-a-tat-tats" and the "thump, thumps." Tell the children they should listen closely because the narrator's voice will also get louder and softer as the parade is entering and leaving town, and they should follow the cue. Mention that the narrator will point to the children when it is their turn to "play their instruments" (say their words). Remind them that they must watch closely to know when it is their group's turn. Have the "rat-a-tat-tat" group form one column, the "thump, thump" group a second column, and then ask them to march in place. Then, the narrator, as drum major, reads the story, and the fun begins! The musical experiences include marching to music, repeating a refrain, and learning a beat.

RECOMMENDATIONS

The figurative language makes this an excellent book to share with all ages of children. It contains similes and personification as well as onomatopoeia. There is a natural art extension as the musicians are completely comprised of various shapes. Children can take shape patterns and make their own rows of figures.

ADDITIONAL EXTENSION

Have a real parade with the children marching around the room. Use flags, rhythm instruments, song flutes, and horns (remember, instruments with mouthpieces should never be shared unless they are sanitized). Play a stirring march tune or a song specifically written for rhythm music accompaniment.

We All Sing with the Same Voice
J. Philip Miller and Sheppard M. Greene;
illustrated by Paul Meisel
(HarperCollins)

This *Sesame Street* song was originally recorded by *The Sesame Street* house band in 1982 and first aired on *Sesame Street* during its fourteenth season. The song celebrates the fact that children from different countries, who look and act dissimilar, are all the same in some ways and in other ways are in harmony (different, but able to blend together nicely). Bright, colorful, childlike illustrations depict children joyfully singing together.

EXTENSION: **Multicultural Dances and Harmony**

MATERIALS

> tape or CD player
> musical recording of multicultural dances

PROCEDURE

Music for this *Sesame Street* song can be found in *The Sesame Street Songbook*.[1] Children should be able to learn the chorus and sing along. Because the phrase "And we sing in harmony" repeats several times in the text, this is the perfect time to teach children the concept of harmony. This can be done using a keyboard, chimes, or a xylophone. For example, play the note G at the same time you play the note E, and note the pleasant effect. Contrast this with the combination of B and A,

which is disharmonious. The book also lends itself well to teaching children music or dances from other countries. Two easy dances to teach children that they should enjoy are the "Mexican Hat Dance" and "The Circle Dance." Musical experiences include learning to sing and dancing to music.

RECOMMENDATIONS

You can find music and dance instructions for multicultural dances on the following recordings: Georgiana Stewart's *Children's Folk Dances* and *Folk Dance Fun*, and Pamela Conn Beall and Susan Hagen Nipp's *Wee Sing around the World*. A video with "The Circle Dance" and several other movement and activity songs for kids is available on John Jacobson and Alan Billingsley's *Around the World with Me*.

ADDITIONAL EXTENSIONS

Present two songs from Raffi's *One Light, One Sun* that follow a similar theme. Both "One Light, One Sun" and "Like Me and You" express the closeness and unity of people from many countries around the planet. Have the children discuss what the songs mean to them. As an additional activity, create paper doll cutouts that connect with each other at their hands. One source for making these dolls is *The Kids Can Press Jumbo Book of Easy Crafts*.[2] Have children decorate the dolls to look like themselves. As they are working and to enhance this experience, play the songs again as background music.

What a Wonderful World
George David Weiss and Bob Thiele;
illustrated by Ashley Bryan
(Atheneum)

This song, made famous by Louis Armstrong, is accompanied by very vividly colored tempera and gouache paintings. The children are depicted performing a puppet show that follows the lyrics of the song. The words of the song framing the bottom of each page are painted in calligraphy. Sadly, there is no musical score in the book. This book would be the perfect accompaniment to the picture book above, *We All Sing with the Same Voice*.

EXTENSION: **Playing a Song with Boomwhackers**

MATERIALS

> Boomwhackers (percussion tubes) or eight-note handbells
>
> tape or CD player
>
> musical recording of "What a Wonderful World" by Louis Armstrong

PROCEDURE

Even young children can easily learn to sing this song when you add simple motions and show the children the large detailed illustrations in the book. Teach younger children motions first while playing the recording. Older children will be able to learn the words quickly and be able to sing along to the tape or CD. Because *What a Wonderful World* depicts children and puppets from diverse cultures, consider sharing multicultural music after using the book. A favorite song that children will enjoy learning is the African song "A Ram Sam Sam." (*See* figure 4.5.) Because this song is written in a C major scale with no sharps or flats, it is a good song to teach children to play, by

either using eight-note handbells or Boomwhackers. (The most common Boomwhackers for purchase are the eight percussion tubes that comprise a diatonic C major scale. However, you can also purchase chromatic tubes—sharps and flats—and pentatonic scales and so forth. Eight-note handbells and Boomwhackers are available from Music in Motion; *see* "Recommended Musical Catalogs" above.) Musical experiences include using recorded music, acting out a song, and playing instruments.

RECOMMENDATIONS

When using Boomwhackers with children, mention that they are to be used appropriately and responsibly. Children should not hit other children with their Boomwhackers. It is to be treated as an instrument. The children can strike Boomwhackers on their hands, knees, or a table, but we recommend the hands. To make the fullest sound, they need to strike it halfway between the label and the top edge of the Boomwhacker. If cost is a concern, use different-sized cut lengths of one-inch PVC pipe as an alternative. To play these, have children strike the bottoms of the pipes on the palms of their hands.

FIGURE 4.5 ~ "A Ram Sam Sam" Music for *What a Wonderful World*

ADDITIONAL EXTENSIONS

Because this book presents the lyrics as scenes from a puppet show, you might want to have the children make simple puppets and props and perform the song as given in the book. Children can also paint a mural depicting what a wonderful world looks like, which could then be used as a backdrop if doing a puppet show. Another extension is to listen to the recording and then sing "It's a Small, Small World," which can be found on *Five Little Monkeys*. If staging a puppet show, play this song at the beginning of the show.

Who Took the Cookies from the Cookie Jar?
Bonnie Lass and Philemon Sturges;
illustrated by Ashley Wolff
(Little, Brown)

A skunk bakes some chocolate chip cookies and puts them in his cookie jar. Later, he notices they are missing and tries to discover which of his animal friends stole the cookies from the cookie jar. Thus follows the familiar chant with different animals being blamed as the culprits. At the end of the book, the reader discovers ants are to blame, and all the other animals join the ants for a chocolate chip cookie picnic. The illustrations, done in watercolor and pen, depict a southwestern setting.

EXTENSION: Musical Game

MATERIALS

> tape or CD player
> musical recording of "Who Took the Cookies from the Cookie Jar?"

PROCEDURE

A natural progression after reading this story is to play the musical game "Who Took the Cookies from the Cookie Jar?" Directions for a version of this game are detailed on the front endpapers of the book. It differs from the traditional game because the characters of the story are used instead of children's names. You may wish to have children play the traditional game first and then

follow with this book's animal version of the game. Consult Pamela Conn Beall and Susan Hagen Nipp's *Wee Sing and Play* or *Six Little Ducks* for the traditional version of the song. Another print version of this chant that is manipulative (the cookie jar lid lifts up and down) is *Who Stole the Cookies from the Cookie Jar?* by Jane Manning. Musical experiences include chanting, learning rhythm or beat, repeating refrains, and playing a musical game.

RECOMMENDATIONS

Because this book is set in the southwestern United States, it has some animals that might not be recognizable to young children who live in different parts of the world. You might want to talk about the animals, what they eat, the flora of the area, and other background details in the rich illustrations. An observant reader will notice that subtle clues on the preceding page tell which animal will be revealed next.

ADDITIONAL EXTENSIONS

The surprise ending of this book discloses that the ants took the cookies from the cookie jar. For fun, connect your additional extensions to ants. Sing the song "The Ants Go Marching One by One," contained in Lorna Philpot and Graham Philpot's delightful flap songbook *Amazing Anthony Ant* (out of print but possibly available at libraries). For a math connection, present Elinor Pinczes's *One Hundred Hungry Ants*. Finally, to test children's skills at observation, read Chris Van Allsburg's *Two Bad Ants*.

Zin! Zin! Zin! A Violin
Lloyd Moss; illustrated by Marjorie Priceman
(Simon & Schuster)

One by one, instruments are added to an orchestra until the entire orchestra is assembled on the stage. Children are introduced in this way to the terms *solo, duet, trio,* and so forth, up to *nonet* (nine) and finally the chamber group of ten. This is a wonderful introduction to an orchestra, to musical instruments, and to the concept of counting by using terminology found in music. The text, in rhythm and rhyme, swoops and swirls across the page, reflecting the flow of the music.

EXTENSION: **Making Musical Instruments**

MATERIALS

> clean, empty cylindrical containers
>
> contact or construction paper
>
> wooden spoons (optional)
>
> rubber bands
>
> shoe boxes
>
> clean, empty glass soda or tea bottles
>
> pens or unsharpened pencils
>
> tape or CD player
>
> musical recording of "Rig-a-Jig-Jig"

PROCEDURE

Have children make their own musical instruments. Use oatmeal boxes, coffee cans, or vegetable shortening canisters as drums. Cover them with construction or contact paper. Children can beat on the lids with their hands or a wooden spoon. For "stringed" instruments, stretch rubber bands of various lengths and widths across shoe boxes and strum with fingers. Collect glass soda or tea bottles, and add different levels of water to them as shown in figure 4.6. By striking on the side of each bottle with a pen or pencil, the child can produce various pitches. As an alternative, each child can hold a bottle and blow across the top to create notes that sound like a flute. Make sure the bottle rims are clean and that children are assigned one bottle for sanitary reasons. If they want to switch bottles, clean the rims with

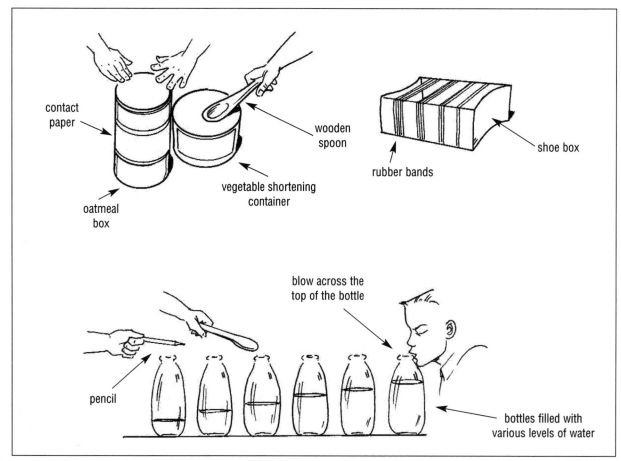

FIGURE 4.6 ~ Instruments for *Zin! Zin! Zin! A Violin*

rubbing alcohol. As a final activity, choose instruments that children can carry, such as standard rhythm instruments. Have them perform the song "Rig-a-Jig-Jig" by marching to the music and following the directions by adding one child and musical instrument at a time. A nice recording can be found on Lynn Kleiner and Cecilia Riddell's *Kids Make Music, Babies Make Music Too!* Musical experiences include making instruments, playing instruments, and marching to music.

RECOMMENDATIONS

Because this book depicts the concepts of solo, duet, trio, and so forth through chamber group, it would be a wonderful discussion starter to teach children an understanding of these terms. Have one child stand up and make a sound for a solo, then add a child at a time with a different sound to explain the other terms. The song "Rig-a-Jig-Jig" also helps to clarify these musical terms.

ADDITIONAL EXTENSION

Because this book provides a splendid introduction to an orchestra, it is a perfect read-aloud before playing orchestral music. A natural extension is to have children identify the four main sections of the orchestra: strings, brass, woodwinds, and percussion. A book and CD that highlight these four sections and then continue with some classic orchestral selections is David Chesky's *Classical Cats*. It can be ordered from the Educational Record Center (*see* "Recommended Musical Catalogs" above). A book that introduces the various instruments of the orchestra with detailed pictures is *Meet the Orchestra,* by Ann Hayes. Another good introduction to the orchestra can be found at the beginning of the Disney video *Fantasia*.

Notes

1. *The Sesame Street Songbook: Sixty-Four Favorite Songs* (New York: Collier, 1994), 47–49.

2. Judy Ann Sadler, *The Kids Can Press Jumbo Book of Easy Crafts,* illus. Caroline Price (Tonawanda, N.Y.: Kids Can Press, 2001), 144.

Bibliography of Picture Books Used in Music Extensions

Aylesworth, Jim. *Old Black Fly.* Stephen Gammell, illus. New York: Henry Holt, 1992.

Baer, Gene. *Thump, Thump, Rat-a-Tat-Tat.* Lois Ehlert, illus. New York: HarperCollins, 1989.

Bang, Molly. *When Sophie Gets Angry—Really, Really Angry . . .* New York: Scholastic, 1999.

Birdseye, Tom, and Debbie Holsclaw Birdseye, adapters. *She'll Be Comin' Round the Mountain.* Andrew Glass, illus. New York: Holiday House, 1994.

Carle, Eric. *Papa, Please Get the Moon for Me.* New York: Simon & Schuster, 1986.

Carter, David A. *If You're Happy and You Know It.* New York: Scholastic, 1997.

Crebbin, June. *Cows in the Kitchen.* Katharine McEwen, illus. Cambridge, Mass.: Candlewick, 1998.

Galdone, Paul. *Cat Goes Fiddle-I-Fee.* Boston: Houghton Mifflin, 1988.

Garcia, Jerry, and David Grisman. *Teddy Bears' Picnic.* Bruce Whatley, illus. New York: HarperCollins, 1996. (Book and cassette ed.).

Gershwin, George, Dubose Heyward, Dorothy Heyward, and Ira Gershwin. *Summertime.* Mike Wimmer, illus. New York: Simon & Schuster, 1999.

Hayes, Ann. *Meet the Orchestra.* Karmen Thompson, illus. San Diego, Calif.: Harcourt Brace, 1991.

Hort, Lenny. *The Seals on the Bus.* G. Brian Karas, illus. New York: Henry Holt, 2000.

Jorgensen, Gail. *Crocodile Beat.* Patricia Mullins, illus. New York: Bradbury, 1989.

Kennedy, Jimmy. *The Teddy Bears' Picnic.* Michael Hague, illus. New York: Henry Holt, 2002.

Kerley, Barbara. *The Dinosaurs of Waterhouse Hawkins.* Brian Selznick, illus. New York: Scholastic, 2001.

Kirk, Daniel. *Hush Little Alien.* New York: Hyperion, 1999.

Lass, Bonnie, and Philemon Sturges. *Who Took the Cookies from the Cookie Jar?* Ashley Wolff, illus. Boston: Little, Brown, 2000.

Manning, Jane. *Who Stole the Cookies from the Cookie Jar?* New York: HarperCollins, 2001.

McNaughton, Colin. *Here Come the Aliens!* Cambridge, Mass.: Candlewick, 1995.

Miller, J. Philip, and Sheppard M. Greene. *We All Sing with the Same Voice.* Paul Meisel, illus. New York: HarperCollins, 2001.

Moss, Lloyd. *Zin! Zin! Zin! A Violin*. Marjorie Priceman, illus. New York: Simon & Schuster, 1995.

Nikola-Lisa, W. *Bein' with You This Way*. Michael Bryant, illus. New York: Lee & Low, 1994.

Oppenheim, Joanne. *You Can't Catch Me*. Boston: Houghton Mifflin, 1986.

Paxton, Tom. *Going to the Zoo*. Karen Lee Schmidt, illus. New York: Morrow, 1996.

Philpot, Lorna, and Graham Philpot. *Amazing Anthony Ant*. New York: Random House, 1994.

Pinczes, Elinor. *One Hundred Hungry Ants*. Boston: Houghton Mifflin, 1993.

Raffi. *Wheels on the Bus*. New York: Crown, 1990.

Rodgers, Richard, and Oscar Hammerstein II. *My Favorite Things*. Renee Graef, illus. New York: HarperCollins, 2001.

Rounds, Glen. *Old MacDonald Had a Farm*. New York: Holiday House, 1989.

Shields, Carol Diggory. *Saturday Night at the Dinosaur Stomp*. Scott Nash, illus. Cambridge, Mass.: Candlewick, 1997.

Van Allsburg, Chris. *Two Bad Ants*. Boston: Houghton Mifflin, 1988.

Van Laan, Nancy. *Possum Come a-Knockin'*. George Booth, illus. New York: Knopf, 1990.

Weiss, George David, and Bob Thiele. *What a Wonderful World*. Ashley Bryan, illus. New York: Atheneum, 1995.

Whippo, Walt. *Little White Duck*. Bernard Zaritzky, musician. Joan Paley, illus. Boston: Little, Brown, 2000.

Zelinsky, Paul O. *The Wheels on the Bus*. New York: Dutton, 2000.

Bibliography of Musical Recordings and Videos Used in Music Extensions

Bartels, Joanie. *Dancin' Magic*. Van Nuys, Calif.: Discovery Music, 1991.

Beall, Pamela Conn, and Susan Hagen Nipp. *Wee Sing*. Los Angeles: Price Stern Sloan, 1981.

_____. *Wee Sing and Play*. Los Angeles: Price Stern Sloan, 1998.

_____. *Wee Sing around the World*. Los Angeles: Price Stern Sloan, 1998.

Chesky, David. *Classical Cats: A Children's Introduction to the Orchestra*. New York: Chesky Records for Kids, 1997.

Disney, Walt. *Walt Disney's Masterpiece Fantasia*. Burbank, Calif.: Buena Vista Home Video, 2000.

Five Little Monkeys. Long Branch, N.J.: Kimbo, 2000.

Gershwin, George. *Porgy and Bess*. Universal City, Calif.: MCA Records, 1992.

Greg and Steve. *On the Move with Greg and Steve*. Cypress, Calif.: Youngheart Music, 1998.

_____. *We All Live Together, Volume 2*. Cypress, Calif.: Youngheart Music, 1979.

_____. *We All Live Together, Volume 3*. Cypress, Calif.: Youngheart Music, 1979.

Jacobson, John, and Alan Billingsley. *Around the World with Me: Movement and Activity Songs with Kids*. Milwaukee, Wis.: Hal Leonard, 1988.

Kindergarten Hits. Swanton, Vt.: Kidzup, 2001.

Kleiner, Lynn, and Cecilia Riddell. *Kids Make Music, Babies Make Music Too!* Miami: Warner Brothers, 1998. (CD with same title by Music Rhapsody, 1998).

Murphy, Jane, and Dennis Buck. *Once upon a Dinosaur*. Long Branch, N.J.: Kimbo, 1987.

Palmer, Hap. *Rhythms on Parade*. Freeport, N.Y.: Educational Activities, 1989.

Raffi. *One Light, One Sun*. Willowdale, Ont.: Troubadour Records, 1985.

_____. *Singable Songs for the Very Young*. Willowdale, Ont.: Troubadour Records, 1985.

Rodgers, Richard, and Oscar Hammerstein II. *The Sound of Music*. New York: BMG Entertainment, 1995.

Rosen, Gary. *Teddy Bears' Picnic*. Brattleboro, Vt.: GMR Records, 1999.

Six Little Ducks. Long Branch, N.J.: Kimbo, 1997.

Stewart, Georgiana. *Children's Folk Dances*. Long Branch, N.J.: Kimbo, 1998.

_____. *Folk Dance Fun: Simple Folk Songs and Dances*. Long Branch, N.J.: Kimbo, 1984.

Where Is Thumbkin? Long Branch, N.J.: Kimbo, 1998.

Music Resource Books

Bayless, Kathleen M., and Marjorie E. Ramsey. *Music: A Way of Life for the Young Child*. New York: Macmillan, 1991.

Burton, Stephanie K. *Music Mania*. Manitou Springs, Colo.: Panda Bear, 1994. (Available from Music in Motion, <http://www.musicmotion.com>).

Hart, Avery, Paul Mantell, and Loretta Trezzo Braren. *Kids Make Music! Clapping and Tapping from Bach to Rock*. Charlotte, Vt.: Williamson, 1993.

Kleiner, Lynn, and Cecilia Riddell. *Kids Make Music, Babies Make Music Too!* Miami: Warner Brothers, 1998. (CD with same title by Music Rhapsody, 1998).

Marino, Jane. *Sing Us a Story: Using Music in Preschool and Family Storytimes*. New York: H. W. Wilson, 1994.

McDonald, Dorothy T. *Music in Our Lives: The Early Years*. Washington, D.C.: National Assn. for the Education of Young Children, 1979.

Moomaw, Sally. *More than Singing: Discovering Music in Preschool and Kindergarten*. St. Paul, Minn.: Redleaf, 1997.

Schiller, Pam, and Thomas Moore. *Where Is Thumbkin? 500 Activities to Use with Songs You Already Know*. Beltsville, Md.: Gryphon House, 1994.

Silberg, Jackie. *The I Can't Sing Book for Grownups Who Can't Carry a Tune in a Paper Bag . . . But Want to Do Music with Young Children*. Beltsville, Md.: Gryphon House, 1998.

Wirth, Marian, Verna Stassevitch, Rita Shotwell, and Patricia Stemmler. *Musical Games, Fingerplays, and Rhythmic Activities for Early Childhood*. West Nyack, N.Y.: Parker, 1983.

Chapter Five

Extending Picture Books through Math

Mathematics is the language with which God has written the universe.

— Galileo Galilei

Although you *might* be able to proceed through a day without engaging in art, drama, or music, one could argue legitimately that *everyone* relies on math *every* day. From the time we choose to wake up in the morning on a particular day to the size of our clothing, how long we heat our morning beverages, the speed at which we travel to work or school, the shapes of the road signs we pass, how we portion the hours of our day, the cost of any purchases made and the payment method involved in those transactions, and the number of people with whom we interact—all relate to mathematical concepts. These all-important math skills can be developed using picture books with young children.

MATHEMATICAL SKILLS

Children move through stages in their understanding of number concepts, from concrete (hands-on), to symbolic (the adult first, and then

the child, adds numerals to these concrete experiences), and finally to abstract (the child is able to work exclusively with numerals). During early childhood, children can learn a number of key universal mathematical processes. First, an understanding and sense of numbers must be practiced, developed, and incorporated into rote counting. Rote counting begins as memorization. Learning to count is an important part of language development. Attaching meanings (quantities) to those number words results in number sense. Children learn through repetition, by counting how many steps it is to walk to the mailbox, or a neighbor's house, or the end of the block, and so forth. Children love large numbers, so capitalize on this enthusiasm. As soon as they have mastered the numerals zero through five, and then six through nine, they are ready for information about place value as they begin to string these numerals together.

Children have many numbers that are unique to them and therefore special. The important numbers of an address or telephone number can be learned by singing them, ad nauseam, to the tune of a known song such as "Frere Jacques" or "Twinkle, Twinkle, Little Star." Children's weight in pounds (or kilograms) and ounces and height in feet (or centimeters) and inches are other fascinations for many children, especially as these numbers increase throughout the year.

One-to-one correspondence develops as children learn to touch and count actual objects, matching each object to a spoken number. Children count the fingers on their hands, the candles on their cakes, and their steps up and down the stairs, going forward and back down in counting as they use them. Counting on a calendar not only provides practice of one-to-one correspondence, but also aids in learning the numerals to thirty in order. Children who have difficulty with one-to-one correspondence may be encouraged to "push and count" each item by separating it from the others. Handing out napkins, one to each child, at snack time, is another of a myriad of practical experiences that aids children in this concept. As children become better at counting, pictures of things to count may replace these objects, and illustrated books with natural math extensions provide these pictures. Many of these books help children learn to match a set of objects to the correct numeral, readying them for future use of these sets to perform number operations.

Today's early childhood classrooms, and even children's museums, are full of hands-on activities for the purpose of learning mathematical concepts (not solely for operations with numbers, but also for discovery of size, weight, volume, spatial relationships, and so forth). Patterning, which is so important throughout mathematics, has as its basis the language of classification. Parents can help prepare children for success in school by reading to them and talking with them about what they are doing. Both of these activities provide important language acquisition for young children that they will need as they learn to sort by color, shape, size, and additional attributes. For example, pairing the family's socks after they have been laundered provides children with practice in sorting by color and size; watching for road signs to discuss while riding; using relevant information from cereal boxes, magazines, mail, and so forth in conversations—all these lead to language acquisition skills and school success.

Number operations of addition, subtraction, multiplication, and division are the essential manipulations of numerals that allow daily problem solving in our lives. Children learn through trial and error, as well as instruction, which processes are necessary in a variety of real-life situations. Young children group sets to represent the quantities, then combine these groups and recount the totals, or remove amounts to find the difference, draw their results, and finally progress to substituting numerals for these amounts.

The great Leonardo da Vinci, painter, engineer, musician, and scientist from the fifteenth and sixteenth centuries, stated, "Let proportion be found not only in numbers and measures, but also in sounds, weights, times, and positions, and what ever force there is." It is surprising to think that children who are playing with blocks are engaged in geometry, those playing hide-and-seek are also learning algebra as they search for what is missing by using clues and eliminating possibilities, and those engaged in throwing balls are laying the groundwork for trigonometry. *Play is a child's work.* It is their job to figure out how the world works, and math is an important part of that process. Children *need* to handle shapes, sizes, and mass; to pour rice and sand and water from one container to another; and to have predictable times in their schedules. Besides, math is fun for all ages!

MATH TIPS

The term *number* refers to an actual amount of objects, but use *numeral* to designate the written symbol for this. For example, we could say the crows on the telephone wire numbered twenty, but when we refer to *20,* it is a numeral. This distinction is necessary because learning accurate language now allows for easier communication of ideas as youngsters move into more sophisticated mathematics.

Note that, with the various font types in which numerals appear, children may not always recognize some of them. And when children print numerals, reversals are natural and may be dealt with in the breezy, matter-of-fact manner of "Whoops—that seven needs to go the other way."

Finally, when we read numerals in the hundreds, we reserve the use of *and* to those times when we are reading a decimal point. We avoid saying *and* between the hundreds and tens. For instance, "104" is read simply "one hundred four," while "104.2" is said as "one hundred four *and* two-tenths." This is important especially when children read amounts of money with decimal points, and it prevents confusion when hearing numerals said aloud.

EXPLANATIONS OF MATH CONCEPTS

Although children will be in different stages of mathematical maturity, and some may not as easily follow the numerical discussion, all children can begin to grab onto the concepts and the language used to discuss them. The following common math concepts are incorporated into our activities.

Classification—Sorting objects based on one or more attributes, including color, shape, size, texture, or any other properties

Counting—Includes rote counting of cardinal numbers (one, two, three . . .) and ordinal numbers (first, second, third . . .) as well as counting by twos, fives, tens, and other multiples and "counting on," in which children count a group of objects and then continue from that total when an additional group of objects is added, without needing to start at one again

Fraction—Denotes a portion by containing a numerator, or top or first number, which tells how many parts of the divided whole are included, and a denominator, or bottom or second number, which tells into how many pieces the whole has been divided. If three-fourths of a circle has been shaded, it means three out of the four parts, or three-quarters, are indicated.

Measurement—Using standard units to determine length or distance, weight or mass, volume or capacity, time and speed

Number—A quantity, often found by counting or completing a mathematical operation

Number Sense—The ability to see at a glance how many of a small number of objects are present and whether one pile has more, less, or the same quantity compared to another group. It allows the learner to estimate an approximate answer. Number sense is reached after many exposures to manipulatives (hands-on mathematical props, such as colored wooden cubes) and the experience of free as well as guided play, when a certain level of mental maturation is reached.

Numeral—The written figure that represents the number

One-to-One Correspondence—Allows the knowledgeable child to say one numeral for each object that is being counted, without skipping any objects—while physically or mentally touching each piece once, and only once, as they count—nor saying two numerals for only one object

Ordering—Arranging items in a reasonable way, based on set criteria such as size (e.g., from largest to smallest)

Patterns—Repetitions in the same order, labeled by letters of the alphabet for each repeating section. A red and white stripe would be labeled an *AB* pattern, while a red, white, and blue stripe is called *ABC*. Patterns may also increase, as in *AB, ABB, ABBB,* and so forth.

Problem Solving—Comprehending words, either oral or written, and knowing what operation(s) to perform to obtain the correct answer

Quantity—Amount, whether it is based on a measurement or on the results of a number operation, such as a sum in addition, a difference in subtraction, a product in multiplication, or a quotient in division

Shapes—Dimensional forms. Those commonly learned in early childhood include two-dimensional circles, squares, stars, triangles, rectangles, ovals, diamonds, hearts, hexagons, and perhaps crescents; and three-dimensional spheres (balls), cones (as in ice cream), cubes (boxes, blocks), and any others that a child can reference, such as pyramids. A high school math teacher once mentioned to us that early childhood classes should use proper terminology; a diamond should be taught as a rhombus and an oval be referred to as an ellipse. The reader can decide on correct and appropriate terminology.

Size and Weight—Measurements of physical properties: *size* refers to the linear amount of space taken up; *weight* refers to an object's heaviness

Spatial Relationships—Three-dimensional views of forms from a variety of perspectives. Vocabulary that describes where something is placed in respect to other forms is of paramount importance for language development and for the purpose of understanding and following directions (*see* words listed under "Position" below).

Time and Money—Invented measurements used to provide order to our days, weeks, months, and years or to aid in bartering for the goods or services

we need in exchange for the goods or services that we can provide. Ambrose Bierce, author of *The Devil's Dictionary* (Oxford University Press, 1998), defined money as a blessing that is of no advantage to us excepting when we part with it, an evidence of culture, and a passport to polite society.

Language Development Terms Associated with Math

Mathematics has a vocabulary of its own beyond *add, subtract, multiply,* and *divide*. The following words, necessary for sorting and classifying, are commonly used by the public. Many of them will appear in the print soon to be read and written by the young child, so they are especially useful to know.

Age—Young, middle-aged, old

Colors—Red, orange, yellow, green, blue, purple, brown, white, black, gray, pink; progressing to finer distinctions, such as violet, maroon, tan, beige, etc.

Composition—Liquid, solid, dry, wet, dense, porous, utility, wood, metal, man-made, natural

Number—More, less, the same, many, few, one, first, second, etc.

Position (Direction, Relationship)—Near, far, above, below, left, right, front, back, in, out, on, off, under, over, low, high, before, after, top, middle, bottom, around, through, beside, away, here, there, start, end or finish, up, down, forward, backward, first, next, last

Shape—In addition to those named above under "Explanations of Math Concepts," wide, narrow, thick, thin

Size—Big or large, little or small, medium

Sound—Loud, soft or quiet, fast, slow, high-pitched, low-pitched

Speed—Fast, slow, moderate

Temperatures—Hot, cold, warm, cool, room temperature

Texture—Shiny, dull, rough, smooth, hard, soft, grit (of sandpaper), grain (of wood)

Time—Now, later, soon, begin or start, end or finish

This list provides a beginning but is not meant to be all-inclusive. Add to it as dictated by the children's needs and interests. Now, with these ideas in mind, let us explore connections between literature and mathematics.

MATH EXTENSIONS

Bats around the Clock
Kathi Appelt; illustrated by Melissa Sweet
(HarperCollins)

Enter the world of American Batstand—a twelve-hour rock-and-roll party with host Click Dark and some of the jazziest bats you have ever seen. As each hour is depicted on a clock face held by a mouse, the bats begin another type of dance, from the twist to the "bugaloo." Special performers are Chubby Checkers and a bat wearing blue suede shoes. Never has an illustrator who uses watercolors been able to make bats look so appealing.

EXTENSION: **Telling Time**

MATERIALS

>   poster board
>
>   colored markers
>
>   brads
>
>   safety scissors
>
>   pencil

PROCEDURE

While the storyteller is sharing the book, one child can stand at the front of the group and turn the hands of a large clock provided by the reader. (A

sturdy clock with gears that keeps correct hour to minute hand relationships called a Judy Clock is available from Childcraft at <http://www.child craft.com> or 800-631-5652.) Then, have children make their own clocks to take home to use. To make a clock face, trace a circle on a piece of poster board that is large enough that they can use the leftover scraps to make two hands for the clock. Cut out the circle, one hour hand, and one minute hand. Mark the center of the circle with a pencil; poke a brass brad first through the two hands and then through the center. Spread the brad prongs in the back and fold them down. Spin the hands of the clock around in a full circle to make the hole for each hand large enough to spin freely. Use colored markers to add the numerals on the clock face to represent the twelve hours. Mark the top and bottom (12 and 6), then the quarter sides (9 and 3), and finally fill in the two numerals between each of these anchor points (1, 2, 4, 5, 7, 8, 10, and 11). Math concepts include numerals, ordering, and telling time.

RECOMMENDATIONS

The adult may make a model of the clock face circle and fold it in fourths. Where the two lines intersect is the center of the circle. Notch holes for each hour on the outside edge and punch a hole at the center point so the children can quickly mark the centers of their clock faces as well as marks for the hours on the outside edges. Older children may use colored markers to add lines to represent the minutes on the clock face. To save time, the adult may distribute paper plates to make the clock faces rather than having the children trace and cut their own circles.

ADDITIONAL EXTENSION

Several dances are mentioned in this book, and children will enjoy trying some of the dances the bats enjoyed. Teach the children steps for those dances you know (e.g., the shrug, jitterbug, swim, locomotion, twist, and "The Hokey Pokey"). If you do not know how to do some of the dances, have the children make up steps or ask a dance instructor or physical education teacher.

Big Fat Hen
Keith Baker
(Harcourt Brace)

The well-known nursery rhyme "One, Two, Buckle Your Shoe" is accompanied by large, gloriously colored acrylic illustrations that will be very appealing to young children. A clever child will find several items to count on each page.

EXTENSION: **Making a Book of Pairs**

MATERIALS

      construction paper

      safety scissors

      stapler

      ink pad

      crayons or colored markers

PROCEDURE

An adult makes the books for each child ahead of time. Fold a piece of construction paper into thirds. With the paper still folded in thirds, fold it in half with open edges to the side as shown in figure 5.1. Staple the spine of the book, and then cut the folds so that you have a book with six pages. Have children place two fingers on an ink pad, and place two ovals (for eggs) on the left-hand side of the first page of the book. On the following pages, have them continue placing the correct number of eggs (ovals) on the left-hand side of the page, but place them in pairs (two fingerprints, two more fingerprints, etc., in rows). On the right-hand side, the adult can write the corresponding rhyme from the text. Children can then draw a picture of the object next to the rhyme. On the last page of the book, discuss what else comes in pairs (as the two ovals), for example, eyes, legs, gloves, earrings, arms, hands. They can draw objects that come in pairs on the last page. (*See* figure 5.1 for completed book.) Math concepts include counting on, counting by pairs, and patterning.

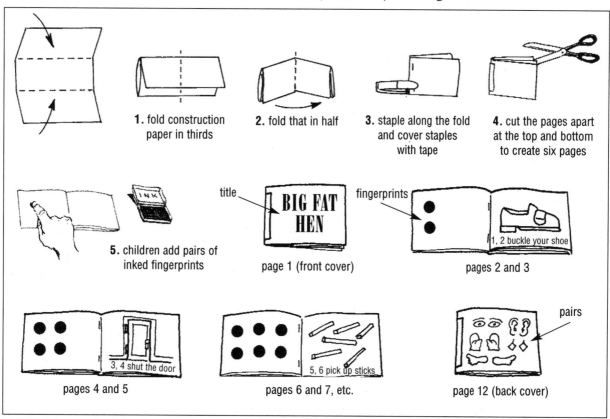

1. fold construction paper in thirds

2. fold that in half

3. staple along the fold and cover staples with tape

4. cut the pages apart at the top and bottom to create six pages

5. children add pairs of inked fingerprints

title — BIG FAT HEN

page 1 (front cover)

fingerprints — 1, 2 buckle your shoe

pages 2 and 3

3, 4 shut the door

pages 4 and 5

5, 6 pick up sticks

pages 6 and 7, etc.

pairs

page 12 (back cover)

FIGURE 5.1 ~ Book for *Big Fat Hen*

RECOMMENDATIONS

Cover the staples on the spine of the book with tape so that children do not get caught on the staples. If the children have time, and are able, they can make the books themselves. To fold paper in thirds, instruct the children to make the paper give itself a "hug." Demonstrate how one side folds across the body, followed by the other side; then the paper is flattened. Paper may be folded either lengthwise or widthwise first, before folding again. Either way will yield six pages; they will simply have different rectangular measurements. Make a copy of the lines of the rhyme for each child. They can cut and paste the words themselves or with an adult's help.

ADDITIONAL EXTENSIONS

Have children share their books of pairs with their families or another audience and talk about how they made them. For example, contact a local retirement home and arrange for an audience so that the children can share their books of pairs. Also, share the book *What's a Pair? What's a Dozen?* by Stephen R. Swinburne. If some of the dialogue is too difficult for your group of children, adjust it accordingly.

The Biggest, Best Snowman
Margery Cuyler; illustrated by Will Hillenbrand
(Scholastic)

Big Mama, Big Sarah, Big Lizzie, and Little Nell all live together in a big house in a big snowy woods. All her sisters and mother tell Little Nell that she is too small to help with anything. When Little Nell goes into the woods to play with her animal friends, they convince her that she is not too small to make a very large snowman. And, it turns out that Little Nell is able to make the biggest, best snowman ever made. Illustrator Hillenbrand used a mixture of mediums (oils, oil pastels, egg tempera, watercolors, water-soluble artist crayons, and pencil) for the snowy winter scenes.

EXTENSION: **Snowman Paper Chain**

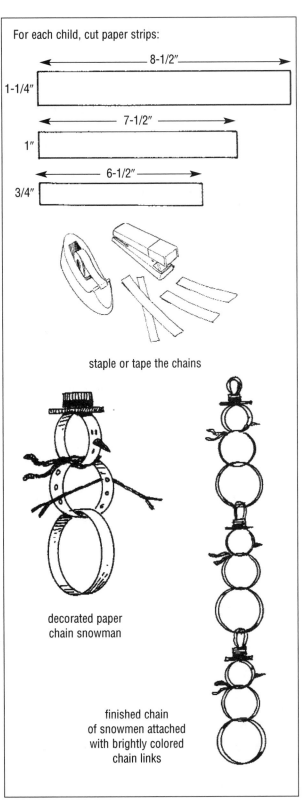

For each child, cut paper strips:

8-1/2"

1-1/4"

7-1/2"

1"

6-1/2"

3/4"

staple or tape the chains

decorated paper chain snowman

finished chain of snowmen attached with brightly colored chain links

FIGURE 5.2 ~
Paper Chain Snowman for *The Biggest, Best Snowman*

MATERIALS

> copier paper
>
> tape or stapler
>
> colored markers
>
> yarn, ribbon, or material strips
> (optional)

PROCEDURE

Cut three paper strips for each child from copier paper. The strip for the bottom of the snowman should be 1 1/4 inches wide by 8 1/2 inches long; the middle strip should be 1 inch wide by 7 1/2 inches long; the top strip should be 3/4 inch wide by 6 1/2 inches long. Children select one strip of each size to make a three-link snowman as shown in figure 5.2. Have the children order the pieces by size and then staple or tape the strips in order with the largest forming the bottom to make one paper chain snowman. They can add marker decorations for the face and tie a strip of yarn, ribbon, or material around the neck area. After each child has completed a snowman, the adult may choose to loop additional strips of a brightly colored paper through each end circle to attach all the snowmen in a long chain to decorate the room. This activity, as well as the concept of the snowman presented in the book, teaches children about classification, specifically, ordering by size, length, and width.

RECOMMENDATIONS

It may be necessary to teach the children how to make a paper chain. Instruct them to loop the paper into a circle before stapling, rather than joining the ends together, which results in a raindrop shape. If there are concerns about young children using the stapler, substitute tape.

ADDITIONAL EXTENSIONS

Share other stories about snow, such as *The Snowy Day,* by Ezra Jack Keats, or *The Mitten* or *The Hat,* by Jan Brett (listed in chapter 3). If it is a snowy day, have the children go outside and make angels or snowmen. If there is no snow, the children can make modeling-dough snowmen (*see The Party*

extension in chapter 2 for a dough recipe). Or make marshmallow snowmen by using two large marshmallows for the body and one small marshmallow for the head, and thread them onto a thin pretzel stick. Features may be added with small candies or licorice.

Bunny Money
Rosemary Wells
(Dial)

Max and Ruby have saved up a walletful of money for Grandma's birthday present and set out to shop for a music box with skating ballerinas. Unfortunately, on the way, they find other ways to spend their money and need to settle for bluebird earrings that play "Oh, What a Beautiful Morning" and a set of glow-in-the-dark vampire teeth. After running out of money, they need to telephone Grandma for a ride home. On the endpapers, bunny money is printed for photocopying purposes so that children have play money to spend. Wells's art includes ink drawings with watercolor painting for this book.

EXTENSION: **Learning the Value of Money**

MATERIALS

> copier paper
>
> photocopier
>
> safety scissors
>
> glue
>
> crayons (optional)
>
> trinkets

PROCEDURE

An adult photocopies the money that is displayed on *Bunny Money*'s endpapers. Children can cut out the money and paste the fronts of the money to the backs (as explained on the last page of the book). They may color their money if they want. Children can use this money to buy trinkets that have already been labeled with prices (prices will need to be in one- and five-dollar amounts as given in the book). Catalogs that sell many trinkets for an inexpensive price include Oriental Trading (call 800-228-2269 or check the web site, <http://www.orientaltrading.com>) or Smile Makers (call 800-825-8085 or go to the web site, <http://www.smilemakers.com>). The latter sells plastic glow-in-the-dark vampire teeth, such as Max bought for Grandma. Math concepts include familiarization with money, problem solving, and numeration, such as adding and subtracting.

RECOMMENDATIONS

If you do not want to purchase trinkets, you can also use empty grocery boxes or cans that have no sharp edges. Or you can purchase pretend food or grocery boxes from an early childhood supply catalog such as Lakeshore (phone 800-421-5354 or check the web site, <http://www.lakeshorelearning.com>) or Childcraft (call 800-631-5652 or order from the web site, <http://www.childcraft.com>).

ADDITIONAL EXTENSION

One of Grandma's presents was a pair of musical earrings. Sing a rollicking rendition of the refrain from the song "Oh, What a Beautiful Morning." For another extension idea, share the half of the book *Twenty-Six Letters and Ninety-Nine Cents*, by Tana Hoban, that deals with money. If possible, have coins available so that children can understand the equivalents displayed in the book. These can be presented to the group by adding magnetic tape to the back of each coin and using a *metal* cookie sheet or other flat metallic surface as the display area.

A Cake All for Me!
Karen Magnuson Beil;
illustrated by Paul Meisel
(Holiday House)

Pig happily mixes up a wonderful chocolate chip cake to eat by himself. Before he can add the chocolate frosting, four friends arrive to share the masterpiece. In addition to being a counting book from one to twenty, the back of the book contains standard measurement equivalents. Children will pore over the detailed illustrations that even label the size of the baking pan—9 inches by 13 inches.

EXTENSION: **Measuring**

MATERIALS

> sand
> 9" x 13" cake pan
> measuring cups
> measuring spoons

PROCEDURE

Fill the cake pan two-thirds full of sand. Have the children use the measuring cups to determine how many quarter cups it takes to fill the one-cup measure, and have them try many of the other measurement equivalents found in the back of the book using the cups and the spoons. Place a drop cloth down on the table for ease of cleanup in case sand is spilled. In addition to measurement, children are also learning the math concept of fractions.

RECOMMENDATIONS

You may also want the children to use water to discover the equivalents for liquid measurements. Provide empty milk cartons of various sizes: half-pint, pint, quart, half-gallon, and gallon. Let children experiment by filling containers with water and seeing how much water it takes for the smaller cartons to fill the larger cartons. Place the book in a resealable plastic bag so the children can pore over the illustrations without pouring water over the pages of the book!

ADDITIONAL EXTENSION

A fun extension is to have the children help measure the ingredients and to produce a tasty treat. No-Bake Cookies is an easy recipe that requires measuring cups and spoons for both liquid and solid ingredients.

NO-BAKE COOKIES

Place the following ingredients in a heatproof pan.

> 2 cups sugar
> 1/2 cup butter
> 1/2 cup milk
> 3 tablespoons of cocoa

Bring to a boil and boil for one minute; then remove from heat. Add the following ingredients.

> 3 cups oatmeal
>
> 1 teaspoon of vanilla
>
> 1/2 cup crunchy peanut butter

Mix well. Drop by spoonful on wax paper. Makes five dozen small cookies. Eat when cool. Store leftovers in a covered container.

Can You Count Ten Toes?
Lezlie Evans; illustrated by Denis Roche
(Houghton Mifflin)

The author presents different items to count on each double-page spread. On the far left side, the numbers are listed in a new language. On the rest of the spread, children need to count the correct number of items using that language. Languages include Spanish, French, Japanese, Chinese, Korean, Tagalog, Russian, Hindi, Hebrew, and Zulu. The last two pages display a small world map and pinpoint the various areas where the individual languages are spoken. Roche's illustrations are gouache on paper.

EXTENSION: An Accordion-Style Counting Book (In Another Language)

MATERIALS

> 1 piece of 12″ x 18″ construction paper per child
>
> safety scissors
>
> glue
>
> fine-tip colored markers
>
> wide-tip colored markers

PROCEDURE

As shown in figure 5.3, the following are directions for children to make an accordion book.

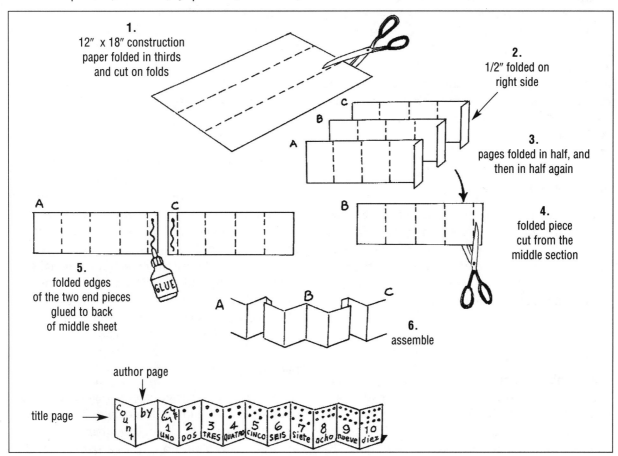

FIGURE 5.3 ~ Accordion Book for *Can You Count Ten Toes?*

Fold construction paper in thirds lengthwise. Cut along the folds to produce three sheets, each 4 inches by 18 inches. Fold down 1/2 inch on the right side of the short end on each piece of paper. Now, stack the three pieces together, and with the folds still intact, fold the remainder of the length in halves, and then in half again to produce fourths. Unfold, and cut the half-inch folded margin off *one* of the three pieces; this will be the middle piece of the accordion fold book. Add glue to the two folded margins, and attach the three sheets together, with the shortest one in the middle, by gluing the half-inch piece to the back of each end of the middle piece. This makes a booklet with twelve pages when folded accordion-style. The first two pages are the title page and author page. The remaining ten pages are used for the numbers one through ten. Making this book would be a wonderful opportunity for cooperative pairs of a younger and older child working together. They can then choose the language they wish to use for their counting book as given in this picture book. The older child can add number words from one to ten in that language on the pages. The younger child could draw or stamp the correct number of objects for each numeral. Math concepts include counting, fractions, and measurement.

RECOMMENDATIONS

The adult can make a poster ahead of time showing the numbers in different languages so that children can copy them. Use wide-tip and fine-tip colored markers if children want to write the symbols in addition to the words, as some symbols require the use of different-width markers.

ADDITIONAL EXTENSION

Use a globe or map of the world to help the children find the various countries where the languages listed in the book are spoken. (*See* the last two pages of the book.) Use removable self-stick colored dots to mark the locations on the globe or map.

Counting Crocodiles
Judy Sierra;
illustrated by Will Hillenbrand
(Harcourt Brace)

Monkey gets tired of eating sour lemons, the only food available on her island. One day she spots a banana tree on a nearby island and decides she wants to go there for a different treat. Unfortunately, she must travel across the Sillabobble Sea, which is filled with hungry crocodiles. She eventually devises a clever plan to hop across the crocodiles' backs while counting them and then double-checking her figures on the way back. The story will be especially appealing to children because of the clever rhymes the monkey uses while counting the crocodiles—for example, "six crocs with pink Mohawks." The story is based on a Pan-Asian trickster folktale. Hillenbrand's illustrations were created in oil, oil pastel, watercolor, and gouache on vellum.

EXTENSION: Counting the "Crocodiles"

MATERIALS

    carpet squares

PROCEDURE

Place carpet squares on the floor a few inches apart, each carpet square depicting a crocodile. Have children walk or hop on the squares one by one and count the number of crocodiles they are hopping over (like the monkey did in the story) until they get to the other side. They then need to count backward until they reach the original side. For each child, add or subtract a few squares so the number of crocodiles is different each time. Math concepts are one-to-one correspondence and counting forward and backward.

RECOMMENDATIONS

Make sure the carpet squares have a rubber backing so the children do not slip. If they do not have that type of backing, have them step on the squares rather than hop, or add strips of rubber grips, found in discount stores, to the back of the carpet squares. Serve bananas or lemonade (as given in the story) when they finish the activity.

ADDITIONAL EXTENSION

Use a crocodile-shaped cookie cutter or a sponge cut in the shape of a crocodile (from an Ellison die) to sponge print on a large sheet of paper. Children can count along and add the descriptive actions of the crocodiles. For sponge printing, fasten a clothespin to the back of the sponge and dip the sponge in paint or onto an ink pad using the clothespin as the handle. Children can have the crocodile shapes wind their way from one end of the paper to the other and draw "islands" at each end.

Eating Fractions
Bruce McMillan
(Scholastic)

McMillan photographed two young children dividing bananas, cloverleaf rabbit rolls, pizza, corn on the cob, strawberry pie, and pear salad into fractions such as halves, thirds, and quarters. Recipes for the rolls, pizza, pear salad, and strawberry pie are included at the back of the book.

EXTENSION: Food Fractions

MATERIALS

> 3 paper circles for each pair of children
> colored markers or crayons
> pencils
> safety scissors

PROCEDURE

To make food fractions, have children work in pairs. Distribute three paper circles to each pair of children. Ask them to decorate them with colored markers or crayons as any of the circular foods given in the story, such as the cloverleaf rabbit roll, pizza pie, wiggle pear salad, or strawberry pie. Then, instruct them to divide the first food item into halves, the second one into thirds, and the third one into fourths. They will want to mark

lines first with a pencil and then cut the pieces. Tell the children to keep a piece of each "food" item for themselves and share extra pieces with another pair of children. Using the extra pieces they obtained, how many combinations of foods can they make into circles? Math concepts include understanding fractions, problem solving, and classification.

RECOMMENDATIONS

To make large circles, which may be easier for young children to handle, fold, and cut, the activity director may use a large dinner plate as a template. For smaller circles use a compass or Ellison die. Children can alternate the tasks of drawing the lines and cutting the pieces.

ADDITIONAL EXTENSION

Serve real foods and have children use their fraction skills to divide them. Two examples are mini pizzas and graham crackers. For mini pizzas, each pair of children splits an English muffin into halves. Each receives a half and then makes his or her own mini pizza by spooning on pizza sauce and a slice of cheese. These can be heated in a toaster oven. Serve graham crackers and have the children divide them into halves and fourths along the scored lines.

Five Creatures
Emily Jenkins; illustrated by Tomek Bogacki
(Farrar, Straus & Giroux)

Five creatures live in a house—three humans and two cats. Then begins a litany of traits that these creatures share in common along with dissimilar traits. The illustrations capably depict some of the similar and different characteristics along with a flowing typeface text explanation. The illustrator is an internationally known painter and illustrator of children's literature.

EXTENSION: Venn Diagram

MATERIALS

> drawing paper

colored pencils, crayons, or markers

safety scissors

1 piece of 12″ x 18″ construction paper per child

2 medium-sized embroidery hoops or 4 chenille stems (pipe cleaners) per child

stapler or glue

PROCEDURE

Read the story to familiarize the children with its content. Have children quickly sketch the five creatures from the book on drawing paper, stressing the size and hair color of each. Have them cut out these creatures. Give children a large sheet of construction paper and two embroidery hoops. Make a Venn diagram by laying the two circles side by side on the construction paper and placing the creatures along the outside. Finally, reread the book, page by page, and have children diagram the results: humans, cats; short, tall; grownups, child; orange hair, gray hair; and so forth. Math concepts include classification, counting, and spatial relationships.

RECOMMENDATIONS

In lieu of using embroidery hoops, two circles for each child may be made from four chenille stems (pipe cleaners). Have them twist together the ends of two pieces of chenille stems to make each circle. The adult demonstrating the diagrams can use hula hoops and enlarged creatures. Older children can extend the original project by choosing a page to illustrate as shown in figure 5.4. They can trace the circles onto construction paper, staple or glue the creatures in place on the background paper, and write a number sentence, for example, 2 + 3 = 5; 2 with gray hair plus 3 with orange hair equals 5 creatures who like birds. (Their finished papers will likely contain most or all of the number families for the sum of five.)

chenille stems

5 creatures who like birds

3 with orange hair + 2 with gray hair

FIGURE 5.4 ～ Venn Diagram for *Five Creatures*

ADDITIONAL EXTENSIONS

Have children talk about the various members of their families and complete family trees. Nina Laden's *My Family Tree* is one of the best books available for children to understand the concept of today's more common nontraditional families. Photocopy a form from this book that every child can use to fill in the blanks for his or her family. There are lines for relatives, and, as in the book *Five Creatures,* there is even space to add pets. Another way to talk about the various types of families is by sharing the song "Family Tree" from the album *Family Tree,* by Tom Chapin.

Grandfather Tang's Story
Ann Tompert; illustrated by Robert Andrew Parker (Crown)

Grandfather Tang and his granddaughter, Little Soo, are entertaining each other by telling stories and making different shapes with their tangram puzzles, ancient Chinese puzzles still used today. A description of how tangrams are used in storytelling is included at the back of the book. The illustrations show how to make each animal character with the seven tangram pieces.

EXTENSION: **Manipulating Tangrams**

MATERIALS

> paper or tangram copies
>
> envelopes
>
> safety scissors

PROCEDURE

There are two different activities you can do with tangrams that correspond to this story. For the first, have pieces of a tangram cut out for each child, and put the pieces into an envelope for easy distribution. Tangrams can be cut with an Ellison die, or you can copy and cut the seven pieces of the tangram square shown in figure 5.5. Ahead of time, make models of the creations from the book, and children can use their pieces to place on top of your models, as if completing a puzzle.

FIGURE 5.5 ~ Tangram for *Grandfather Tang's Story*

For another variation of this extension, children can use the tangram pieces and make an animal as shown in the book. For additional tangram ideas and a printable tangram grid, *see* <http://www.strongmuseum.org/kids/tangram.html>. Math concepts include classification, spatial relationships, and problem solving.

RECOMMENDATIONS

To create a permanent piece of art that records the shapes of the children's tangram creations, have them carefully hold each piece in place and use a crayon to color across the edges onto the paper. When they remove the pieces, the resulting tangram outlines will be displayed.

ADDITIONAL EXTENSIONS

Show children where China is located on a map or globe. Then, share another book about Chinese folklore, such as *The Runaway Rice Cake,* by Ying Chang Compestine. You can also read a story dealing with Chinese culture, for example, Chinese New Year. Two excellent books to share on this topic are *This Next New Year,* by Janet Wong, or *Celebrating Chinese New Year,* by Diane Hoyt-Goldsmith. If you have access to a store that sells

Chinese merchandise, you can purchase Chinese money envelopes and place a penny or dime in each one and give one to each child, explaining the custom of Chinese families giving these money gifts during Chinese New Year. Serve Chinese fortune cookies.

The Grouchy Ladybug
Eric Carle
(HarperCollins)

Children have enjoyed this popular picture book for more than twenty years. Carle uses tissue-paper collages and die-cut pages that fan like an accordion to tell the story of a grouchy ladybug with no manners that thinks she is better than everyone else and that tries to pick a fight with every creature she meets. Children are introduced to the concepts of time, size, and shape along with learning how it is wrong to brag, boast, and pick fights, but better to share.

EXTENSION: **Clock Game**

MATERIALS

white poster board

black marker

tape or CD player

musical recording of "Round in a Circle"

PROCEDURE

As shown in figure 5.6, make twelve poster board squares each approximately one foot square, depending on the size of the poster board, and use a black marker to number them from one to twelve

1. The leader stops the music and announces a time.
2. Children hold up cards from the clock numbers.
3. Inside children stop moving.
4. The two children nearest the numbers make "hands."

Three o'clock!

leader

FIGURE 5.6 ～ Clock Game for *The Grouchy Ladybug*

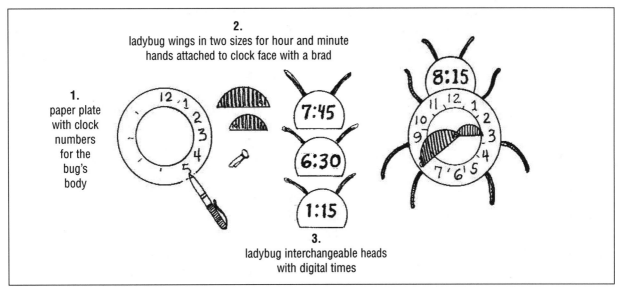

2.
ladybug wings in two sizes for hour and minute
hands attached to clock face with a brad

1.
paper plate
with clock
numbers
for the
bug's
body

3.
ladybug interchangeable heads
with digital times

FIGURE 5.7 ～ Ladybug Clock Face with Interchangeable Heads for *The Grouchy Ladybug*

to represent the numbers found on a clock. Have the children go outside or use a large room. Give each of twelve children a number to hold up, and have them stand in a large circle to form a clock face. Have the rest of the children stand inside the clock face circle. Then, play the song "Round in a Circle," by Greg and Steve, on the recording *We All Live Together, Volume 1*. The children on the inside of the circle walk in a clockwise motion to the music, and the adult stops the recording during the song. Then, the adult calls out a time (in hours) such as three o'clock. The children on the outside of the circle would hold up their signs if they have the numbers twelve and three. The children on the inside of the circle who stopped closest to the twelve and three would hold up their arms to make the clock hands by pointing to their numbers on the clock. Start the music again, and the children on the inside continue marching around the circle until the music stops again. The math concept is telling time. The extension also contributes to number sense.

RECOMMENDATIONS

To vary the person at the twelve o'clock position, who would be raising that sign each time, have the children on the outside circle put down their signs and move ahead to the next hour position

before the music begins again. You can use any musical recording you want, but this song has a repeated refrain for marching around in the circle.

ADDITIONAL EXTENSION

The last part of the book involves telling time to the quarter hour. To practice matching digital time to analog time, use a paper plate to create a clock face as shown in figure 5.7. Make the hands of the clock resemble a ladybug's outer wings (red with black dots). Use white chalk to write various quarter-hour times on black construction paper that has been cut like the head of a ladybug. Position the various heads at the top of the clock and have the children take turns positioning the hands to match each head's digital time.

Jump, Frog, Jump!
Robert Kalan; illustrated by Byron Barton
(Greenwillow)

A cumulative tale about a frog who tries to catch a fly and then becomes the target for others who try to catch him—from a fish, to a snake, to a turtle, and finally to three young boys. Eventually one of the boys decides to release the frog that they caught under a basket. The repetitious refrain, "Jump, frog, jump!" will allow children to join in this participatory tale. The bright greens, blues, and browns, with splashes of yellow, red, orange, and purple used in the illustrations, will intrigue children of all ages.

EXTENSION: Making Patterns

MATERIALS

PROCEDURE

This book has two different patterns: one an add-on in the cumulative rhymes, and the other in the words "Jump, frog, jump!" Observant older children might even notice that the layout of the illustrations is oval, oval, double spread, and then a repeat of that pattern. Also, the snake has a repeated pattern in its skin coloring. Thus, the book would be a good model to teach the concept of patterning. First, have six children design a pattern with body actions, such as *AAB, AAB*. The first *A* child can create a body action such as holding both hands up. The second child would repeat that action. The first *B* child creates a new action, such as hands on knees. The next three children would repeat the pattern displayed by the first three children. Repeat with more sets of children. Then, have the children devise a new pattern. How many patterns can you create? Math concepts include patterns, ordering, and problem solving.

RECOMMENDATIONS

Discuss with the children possible body actions such as hands on head, hands on toes, facing forward or backward, hopping on one foot, and so forth. Cards displaying body actions are available from Math Their Way (Addison Wesley), a program that teaches children the patterns and interconnections in mathematics in a developmentally appropriate way. See their web site, <http://www.center.edu/WORKSHOPS/mtw.html>. Also, the song "The Hokey Pokey" is an example of using body motions in a patterning sequence. Have the children sing and dance "The Hokey Pokey" and talk about the different patterns made after completing the activity.

ADDITIONAL EXTENSIONS

Have children make cereal necklaces with repeated patterns. Bead tan Cheerios and Fruit Loops on string. How many times will the children repeat the pattern? Can they repeat the pattern twice and then do it backward? An example is tan, tan, color; tan, tan, color; color, tan, tan; color, tan, tan. A song you can sing with math concepts of subtracting and counting backward is "Five Little Frogs," also known as "Five Green and Speckled Frogs," available on the recording *Five Little Monkeys*.

Math Curse
Jon Scieszka; illustrated by Lane Smith
(Viking)

Mrs. Fibonacci tells a young girl's math class that almost everything in the world can be thought of as a math problem. The next day, the girl begins to have many math problems and decides that Mrs. Fibonacci has put a math curse on her. After a particularly problematic day (of the math sort), the girl even dreams that night about math problems. The next morning the math curse is broken, but her science teacher, Mr. Newton, exclaims that almost everything is a science experiment, which leads the reader to believe the girl will have a science curse the next day. The zany illustrations and even the design of the book provide numerous math challenges. Even the dedications in the book are math problems to solve. This book is better for second grade and up.

EXTENSION: Math in Everyday Life

MATERIALS

6 large poster boards
colored markers
paper
pencils

PROCEDURE

Ahead of time, an adult prepares six posters, each with one of the following labels: "Time," "Measurement," "Money," "Estimation," "Fractions," and "Problem Solving." Children work independently at the beginning of this extension. Have each child brainstorm ways he or she has used math that day in relation to the six posters and jot these ideas down on paper. This can be done in one large group, or divide the children into six groups and assign one of the above math concepts to each group. Each group will then record all the individual responses for that particular concept. After the groups finish, display the poster board signs and ask all the children if they have any other examples to add to the signs. The math concept is classification.

RECOMMENDATIONS

If this exercise is done early in the day, have children think of examples from the previous day. Feel free to vary the concepts based on group size or time involved.

ADDITIONAL EXTENSIONS

The author named the teacher in the book Mrs. Fibonacci. Fibonacci is actually a math concept that can be explained to children. Cut open an apple to show five seeds inside. Count the vertical lines on a pumpkin. Count the petals on a flower. These are examples of the special Fibonacci numbers that occur in nature and that were discovered by Leonardo Fibonacci during the 1200s. His famous sequence (1, 1, 2, 3, 5, 8, 13, 21, 34, 55, 89, etc.) can be understood by adding 1 plus 1 to equal 2; then adding 1 plus 2 to equal 3, 3 plus 2 to equal 5, and continuing to add the sum of the last addition to the previous number. Also, explore the contributions of Sir Isaac Newton, the English mathematician, because Mr. Newton is the name of the science teacher.

My Little Sister Ate One Hare
Bill Grossman; illustrated by Kevin Hawkes
(Crown)

The narrator's younger sister eats an increasing number of unusual objects such as one hare, two snakes, three ants in underpants, four shrews, five bats, six mice, seven polliwogs, eight worms, and nine lizards. When she eats ten healthy peas, she throws up the whole mess. Hawkes's vibrant and comical illustrations add to the pure "gross factor," which will have children clamoring for the story to be read again and again.

EXTENSION: **Graphing**

MATERIALS

1 piece of 1″ graph paper per child

crayons

PROCEDURE

By beginning at the bottom of the page, have children number up the left-hand side of the graph paper from one to ten. Across the bottom length of the graph paper, they should draw one of each of these items in the following order: hare, snake, ant, shrew, bat, mouse, polliwog, worm, lizard, and a pea. Share the story and then have children fill in their graphs by coloring in the corresponding number of blocks for each item the sister swallows. Math concepts involved are both graphing and patterning.

RECOMMENDATIONS

Instead of drawing each animal, it might be quicker for older children and easier for younger children to have them put the first letter of each animal's name and *p* for *pea* across the bottom of the graph paper. Because two animals begin with *s*, children can list the word *snake* as "sn" or "sk" (because the final sound in a word is easier developmentally for children to hear than a medial sound) and the word *shrew* as "sh". One-inch graph paper (here called Quadrille Ruled Paper) is available from Kurtz Bros., a school supply catalog, which can be reached at 800-252-3811 or edsales@kurtzbros.com.

ADDITIONAL EXTENSIONS

After sharing this story, serve the children gummy worms or other gummy creatures that correspond with the unusual animals that are eaten. For another math concept, have children find and count each set of animals and peas on the last page of the book and then explain the concept of sets. To explain this concept, have children sort buttons into sets by color, size, number of holes, and other characteristics.

One Duck Stuck
Phyllis Root; illustrated by Jane Chapman
(Candlewick)

Down by the marsh, one duck gets stuck in the muck. The repeated refrain, "Help! Help! Who can help?" brings two fish, three moose, four crickets, five frogs, six skunks, seven snails, eight possums, nine snakes, and ten dragonflies to help. With all of them working together, the duck finally is freed. Bright yellows, greens, blues, and browns dominate the gouache pictures.

EXTENSION: **Duck Sets and Subtraction**

MATERIALS

> duck snack crackers
>
> blue construction paper
>
> Baggies

PROCEDURE

After sharing the story, hand each child a piece of blue construction paper to represent a pond and a Baggie containing duck snack crackers. First, have the children create sets with Mama or Papa ducks and babies. They can have one parent duck with two babies, another with four babies, and so forth. Next, have them count the number of ducks in their pond. Present a problem that requires subtracting, an example being that two ducks fly away from the pond. Tell them they can eat two crackers (for the ducks that flew away). How many are left? For this, they can use subtraction skills. Encourage them to now devise their own subtraction problem, eat the appropriate number of crackers, and tell how many they have left. Math concepts include patterning (of the text responses), classification, and subtraction.

RECOMMENDATIONS

If you cannot find duck crackers, you can use fish crackers in the pond or little cheese snack crackers. Make sure that when children are doing their subtraction problems that you tell them they are only to eat a few of the crackers at a time. You can tell a story of baby ducks growing up and leaving the nest, a few at a time. Remind children to wash their hands before eating.

ADDITIONAL EXTENSIONS

Children can make the animals depicted in the story using their fingers and an ink pad. Have them use one or several fingerprints for each animal and then add other details with colored pencils (see the *Bugs! Bugs! Bugs!* extension in chapter 6). Children can count the number of animals they make. Also, children should enjoy singing the song "Five Little Ducks," found on Pam Schiller and Thomas Moore's recording *Where Is Thumbkin?*

One More Bunny
Rick Walton; illustrated by Paige Miglio
(Lothrop, Lee & Shepard)

Simple addition is taught with an increasing number of bunnies coming to a playground area to play. There are rhymed verses on each double-page spread announcing the number of bunnies. Then, different sets that can be added to reach a certain number (e.g., three plus two equals five, and four plus one equals five) are shown on each page. An observant child will realize that sets of objects that correlate with the addition problems can also be found hidden on the page. (Answers are given on the last page.) Miglio has employed colored pencils on watercolor for the lush illustrations.

EXTENSION: **Bunny Math Cards**

MATERIALS

> 10 index cards per child
>
> bunny stamp(s)
>
> ink pad(s)

PROCEDURE

The adult uses a bunny stamp and ink pad to stamp one bunny on each index card. Each child will need ten bunny index cards. After presenting the story, go through the book again and have the children do some of the addition problems using their set of bunny cards. For example, for the number eight, there are four different number families presented to reach the sum of eight and children can do all four by manipulating their bunny cards. Math concepts include addition and classification (sets).

RECOMMENDATIONS

If you have enough bunny stamps and time, let the children stamp their own bunny cards. Children may also round the edges of each card to mimic playing cards. Kidstamps, a distributor of stamps with children's literature characters, has bunny stamps available. To reach Kidstamps, call 800-727-5437 or visit online at <http://www. kidstamps.com>. Alternatively, use pom-poms (which look like bunny tails) to group and count the number families.

ADDITIONAL EXTENSIONS

See the back of the book for other sets that are contained in each illustration and that children can search for and count. Another book to share by the same author and illustrator is *So Many Bunnies,* an ABC and counting book. An additional book using simple addition to reach number families (of seven) is *Quack and Count,* by Keith Baker. For a music extension, have children do "The Bunny Hop."

Over in the Meadow
Jane Cabrera
(Holiday House)

Brilliantly colored child-appealing illustrations that are excellent for group sharing stand out when reading this book, beginning with the bright number and animal blocks on the endpapers. The verses are from a familiar children's song about all the insects and animals that live over in the meadow with their mother. Although the music is not included, most people will know the tune for this song, and it is hard to read this book instead of singing it.

EXTENSION: **One-to-One Correspondence**

MATERIALS

> poster paper (optional)
>
> 1 piece of paper, numbered and labeled, per child
>
> colored dot stickers

PROCEDURE

Make a poster showing the number of babies each animal had or simply hold up the book showing the last two pages, where this is clearly depicted. Give each child a piece of paper with the numbers listed from one to ten along with the names of the mother animals (for graphing setup, *see My Little Sister Ate One Hare*). Have them place the correct number of colored dot stickers to equal the number of babies next to the mom. This is an example of one-to-one correspondence, quantities, and counting concepts.

RECOMMENDATIONS

Match the dot stickers to correspond with the color of the animals listed. Use a green dot for the turtle, yellow dots for the ducks, and so forth, adding details with a pencil or colored markers as necessary (white dots colored gray for the mice and rabbits, yellow and black stripes for the bees, etc.). Or use animal stickers in place of colored dots.

ADDITIONAL EXTENSIONS

Sing a song about a meadow with the words "Down in the meadow in an itty bitty pool . . ." Try "Three Little Fishes," sung by Joanie Bartels on the recording *Bathtime Magic.* Another extension is to play hopscotch, because the endpapers of this book resemble a hopscotch pattern.

Seven Blind Mice
Ed Young
(Philomel)

Young won a 1993 Caldecott Honor award for his artwork accompanying this Indian folktale. From the "ivory tusk" endpapers to the striking black pages and vivid mouse colors, the book's paper collage is graphically pleasing and very eye-catching. Seven blind mice go out to investigate a strange "Something" by their pond. Each day of the week, one of the seven mice reports a different object for the "Something." It is not until Sunday that the last mouse sets out to explore the whole object and discovers it is an elephant.

EXTENSION: **Ordinal Numbers**

MATERIALS

   1″ colored wooden cubes

PROCEDURE

After sharing the story the first time, go through the book again and note the order of the mice's colors. Have children work in groups to place the colored cubes in a line according to which colored mouse was first, second, and so forth. Have children call out the ordinal numbers as they arrange the cubes. Next, have them announce which day of the week goes with which color. What object does each color represent in the story in the perception of the mice? Math concepts include counting and ordering.

RECOMMENDATIONS

If you do not have access to colored cubes, use colored squares of construction paper or other colored manipulatives. After reading the tale, talk about the moral and what it means.

ADDITIONAL EXTENSIONS

Because the mice needed to put all the parts of the knowledge they gained together to understand the whole object, the storyteller can compare this story to putting together a jigsaw puzzle. You can make homemade jigsaw puzzles by laminating posters or pictures from a calendar or magazine (or simply use a cereal box) and cutting them into pieces. As the children assemble the puzzle pieces, have them use position words such as on *top, beside, at the bottom,* and so forth, to describe what they are doing. Compare this vocabulary to the locations of the mice as they explore the elephant in the story. You may also want to share the classic tale of *The Seven Blind Men and the Elephant,* upon which this story is based. (An original picture-book edition is not in print, but the story is available in numerous folklore anthologies.)

Turtle Splash!
Cathryn Falwell
(Greenwillow)

This countdown rhyme begins with ten timid turtles. One turtle is scared off each time and dives into the pond, until there is only one turtle remaining. All ten return to sleep at night by the side of the pond. The author-illustrator uses collages made of a variety of materials glued onto bristol board. The materials include handmade paper, tissue paper, grocery bags, construction paper, and scraps—including small pieces of birch bark—saved from other projects. She also used leaf prints in the pictures and explains in detail how to make leaf prints on the last page of the book.

EXTENSION: **Turtle Race Countdown**

MATERIALS

   10 dome (canning) lids, or one per child

   nail

   hammer

   block of wood or thick padding

   permanent colored markers or acrylic paints (optional)

   tub of water

PROCEDURE

The math concept of counting backward is presented in this book. Discuss all the times we count backward in everyday life, for example, to start a race, to count down to midnight at New Year's, and to send a rocket into space. Then, have a Turtle Race Countdown in a container of water to see how long jar lids (turtles) can stay afloat. Let children decide if they would like to hammer any holes in their lids. These holes help to vary the submersion rates during the race. Vary the number of holes, and leave some lids intact as part of the experiment. To add one or more holes, supervise the children in placing a jar lid (used ones are OK) on top of a block of wood or thick padding. Position the nail on top of the lid and strike it with a hammer. Remove the nail and continue with this process until there are enough lids with holes for each child or until you have at least ten. Allow the children to decorate the lids with permanent colored markers or acrylic paint to appear as turtle shells. Have small groups of children gather around the tub of water with their turtles. Instruct them to carefully place their lids on the surface of the water and gently release them. The race begins! But it is a turtle race, so the one that moves the most slowly—in other words, stays afloat the longest—wins the race. Count down the number of floating lids (ten, nine, eight . . .) as the turtles sink to the bottom of the tub. Math concepts include counting backward, problem solving, one-to-one correspondence, number sense, and quantities.

RECOMMENDATIONS

If there are time constraints or too many children, an adult may prepare the holes in the lids ahead of time. After the children decorate their lids, we recommend holding several races with small groups of children each time. The rest of the children, meanwhile, could be engaged in playing such games as pool or bowling, where the number of objects decreases.

ADDITIONAL EXTENSIONS

Share another book about ponds and animals you would see around the pond, Denise Fleming's *In the Small, Small Pond*. Then, share the information about various flora and fauna that you would see at the pond, as given near the end of

the Falwell title. On the last page of the book, Falwell describes in detail how to make leaf prints because she used leaf prints in her illustrations. Have children try making some of these as shown in her illustrations.

The Very Kind Rich Lady and Her 100 Dogs
Chinlun Lee
(Candlewick)

A very kind rich lady adopts 100 stray dogs one day, and they all live together in a tall house on a hill. The story continues by naming all the dogs, including the 100th dog, Bingo, who was always late. Every day the lady brushes all 100 dogs, searches their coats for fleas, feeds her dogs on 100 plates, fusses over them, talks to them, and calls them by their individual names. The 100 dogs were illustrated with watercolor, ink, and pencil.

EXTENSION: **100th Celebration**

MATERIALS

> collections of 100 items
>
> measuring scales
>
> 100 small food items per child

PROCEDURE

Tell children ahead of time to bring a collection of 100 small items (macaroni, pennies, pebbles, candy) or wear 100 of something (ribbons, buttons, braids). Then, hold a 100th celebration and have children talk about their 100 items. Who has the largest collection of 100 items in size? The heaviest? The longest when arranged in a line? The shortest? What shapes can they make? Now, share the above book and talk about the types of dogs they see in the illustrations and their unusual names. Finally, serve each child 100 small food items, for example, raisins, peanuts, sunflower seeds, semisweet chocolate chips, M&Ms, tiny crackers, coconut flakes, and so forth. Pour each treat into a large bowl and let children count out ten each of ten items or twenty each of five items. Math concepts include numeration (counting) and grouping into sets.

RECOMMENDATIONS

Make sure you are wearing or carrying 100 of something yourself! For the treats, have little Baggies available for them to collect the 100 items, but make sure the children wash their hands first!

ADDITIONAL EXTENSIONS

The dog named Bingo is mentioned numerous times in this story. Share the Bingo song. Recordings are found on *Toddlers Sing Playtime* and on *We All Live Together, Volume 4,* by Greg and Steve. Numerous other books cover the concept of 100, including Joseph Slate's *Miss Bindergarten Celebrates the 100th Day of Kindergarten;* Pam Munoz Ryan's *One Hundred Is a Family;* Elinor J. Pinczes's *One Hundred Hungry Ants;* Margery Cuyler's *100th Day Worries;* Rosemary Wells's *Emily's First 100 Days of School,* and Anne Rockwell's *One Hundred School Days.*

Bibliography of Picture Books
Used in Math Extensions

Appelt, Kathi. *Bats around the Clock.* Melissa Sweet, illus. New York: HarperCollins, 2000.

Baker, Keith. *Big Fat Hen.* San Diego, Calif.: Harcourt Brace, 1994.

_____. *Quack and Count.* San Diego, Calif.: Harcourt Brace, 1999.

Beil, Karen Magnuson. *A Cake All for Me!* Paul Meisel, illus. New York: Holiday House, 1998.

Brett, Jan. *The Hat.* New York: Putnam, 1997.

_____. *The Mitten.* New York: Putnam, 1989.

Cabrera, Jane. *Over in the Meadow.* New York: Holiday House, 1999.

Carle, Eric. *Grouchy Ladybug.* New York: HarperCollins, 1996.

Compestine, Ying Chang. *The Runaway Rice Cake.* Tungwai Chau, illus. New York: Simon & Schuster, 2001.

Cuyler, Margery. *The Biggest, Best Snowman.* Will Hillenbrand, illus. New York: Scholastic, 1998.

_____. *100th Day Worries.* Arthur Howard, illus. New York: Simon & Schuster, 2000.

Evans, Lezlie. *Can You Count Ten Toes? Count to Ten in Ten Different Languages.* Denis Roche, illus. Boston: Houghton Mifflin, 1999.

Falwell, Cathryn. *Turtle Splash! Countdown at the Pond.* New York: Greenwillow, 2001.

Fleming, Denise. *In the Small, Small Pond.* New York: Henry Holt, 1993.

Grossman, Bill. *My Little Sister Ate One Hare.* Kevin Hawkes, illus. New York: Crown, 1996.

Hoban, Tana. *Twenty-Six Letters and Ninety-Nine Cents.* New York: Greenwillow, 1987.

Hoyt-Goldsmith, Diane. *Celebrating Chinese New Year.* Lawrence Migdale, illus. New York: Holiday House, 1998.

Jenkins, Emily. *Five Creatures.* Tomek Bogacki, illus. New York: Farrar, Straus & Giroux, 2001.

Kalan, Robert. *Jump, Frog, Jump!* Byron Barton, illus. New York: Greenwillow, 1981.

Keats, Ezra Jack. *The Snowy Day.* New York: Viking, 1962.

Laden, Nina. *My Family Tree: A Bird's Eye View.* New York: Chronicle, 1997.

Lee, Chinlun. *The Very Kind Rich Lady and Her 100 Dogs.* Cambridge, Mass.: Candlewick, 2001.

McMillan, Bruce. *Eating Fractions.* New York: Scholastic, 1991.

Pinczes, Elinor J. *One Hundred Hungry Ants.* Bonnie Mac Kain, illus. Boston: Houghton Mifflin, 1993.

Rockwell, Anne. *One Hundred School Days.* Lizzy Rockwell, illus. New York: HarperCollins, 2002.

Root, Phyllis. *One Duck Stuck.* Jane Chapman, illus. Cambridge, Mass.: Candlewick, 1998.

Ryan, Pam Munoz. *One Hundred Is a Family.* Benrei Huang, illus. New York: Hyperion, 1994.

Scieszka, Jon. *Math Curse.* Lane Smith, illus. New York: Viking, 1995.

Sierra, Judy. *Counting Crocodiles.* Will Hillenbrand, illus. San Diego, Calif.: Harcourt Brace, 1997.

Slate, Joseph. *Miss Bindergarten Celebrates the 100th Day of Kindergarten.* Ashley Wolff, illus. New York: Dutton, 1998.

Swinburne, Stephen R. *What's a Pair? What's a Dozen?* Honesdale, Pa.: Boyds Mills, 2000.

Tompert, Ann. *Grandfather Tang's Story.* Robert Andrew Parker, illus. New York: Crown, 1990.

Walton, Rick. *One More Bunny: Adding from One to Ten.* Paige Miglio, illus. New York: Lothrop, Lee & Shepard, 2000.

_____. *So Many Bunnies*. Paige Miglio, illus. New York: Lothrop, Lee & Shepard, 1998.

Wells, Rosemary. *Bunny Money*. New York: Dial, 1997.

_____. *Emily's First 100 Days of School*. New York: Hyperion, 2000.

Wong, Janet. *This Next New Year*. Yangsook Choi, illus. New York: Frances Foster, 2000.

Young, Ed. *Seven Blind Mice*. New York: Philomel, 1992.

Bibliography of Musical Recordings Used in Math Extensions

Bartels, Joanie. *Bathtime Magic*. Van Nuys, Calif.: Discovery Music, 2002.

Chapin, Tom. *Family Tree*. Burlington, Vt.: Gadfly, 2001.

Five Little Monkeys. Long Branch, N.J.: Kimbo, 1999.

Greg and Steve. *We All Live Together, Volume 1*. Los Angeles: Youngheart Music, 1975.

_____. *We All Live Together, Volume 4*. Los Angeles: Young-heart Music, 1987.

Rodgers, Richard, and Oscar Hammerstein II. *Rodgers and Hammerstein's "Oklahoma!"* New York: Angel Classics, 2001.

Schiller, Pam, and Thomas Moore. *Where Is Thumbkin?* Long Branch, N.J.: Kimbo, 1993.

Toddlers Sing Playtime. Redway, Calif.: Music for Little People, 1999.

Math Resource Books

Baratta-Lorton, Mary. *Math Their Way*. Lebanon, Ind.: Pearson Learning, 1994.

Copley, Juanita V. *The Young Child and Mathematics*. Washington, D.C.: National Assn. for the Education of Young Children, 2000.

Copley, Juanita V., ed. *Mathematics in the Early Years*. Reston, Va.: National Council of Teachers of Mathematics, 1999.

Kohl, MaryAnn, and Cindy Gainer. *MathArts: Exploring Math through Art for 3 to 6 Year Olds*. Cindy Gainer, illus. Beltsville, Md.: Gryphon House, 1996.

Littlefield, Cindy A. *Real-World Math for Hands-On Fun!* Michael Kline, illus. Charlotte, Vt.: Williamson, 2001.

McGowan, Diane, and Mark Schrooten. *Math Play!* Loretta Braren, illus. Charlotte, Vt.: Williamson, 1997.

Polonsky, Lydia, Dorothy Freedman, Susan Lesher, and Kate Morrison. *Math for the Very Young*. Marcia Miller, illus. New York: John Wiley, 1995.

Schiller, Pam, and Lynne Peterson. *Count on Math: Activities for Small Hands and Lively Minds*. Cheryl Kirk Noll, illus. Beltsville, Md.: Gryphon House, 1997.

Tomczyk, Mary. *Shapes, Sizes and More Surprises*. Loretta Trezzo Braren, illus. Charlotte, Vt.: Williamson, 1996.

VanCleave, Janice. *Janice VanCleave's Play and Find Out about Math: Easy Activities for Young Children*. Michelle Nidenoff, illus. New York: John Wiley, 1998.

Warren, Jean. *1-2-3 Math: Pre-Math Activities for Working with Young Children*. Marion Hopping Ekberg, illus. Everett, Wash.: Warren, 1992.

Chapter Six

~ ~ ~

Extending Picture Books through Science

Anyone who knows young children will agree that "Why?" is a frequent, occasionally exasperating, question. In fact, inquiry is a natural learning style for young children. Most children also enjoy touching and trying new things in their environment. One could infer from this that science, with its questioning and experimenting, is a natural offshoot of their inquisitiveness. Howard Gardner's *Intelligence Reframed* (Basic Books, 2000) now includes the naturalist category as an eighth style of learning. This "nature smart" student learns best by being outside, working with rocks, flora, and fauna. People with this learning style have a curiosity about natural phenomena. They enjoy collections that allow them to categorize plants and animals because of their seemingly innate ability for finding links in nature.

THE SCIENTIFIC METHOD

Young children thrive using hands-on learning in science as well as in other aspects of their cognitive development. Encourage them to carefully observe the world around them as you model by speaking your thoughts aloud: "Do you see . . . ?" "Look at . . ." "What is . . . ?" Follow up with the questioning process: "I wonder why . . . ?" "What would happen if . . . ?" "How does . . . ?" Challenge them to guess what the outcome might be. Then, perform explorations as appropriate.

As children compare the results of their experiments to what they thought might happen, and then communicate these orally, through pictures, or in writing, they may find that their curiosity is again aroused and that they have more questions to pursue based on their findings. These inquiries, in turn, will guide you in helping them continue to expand their scientific knowledge in future activities. This teaches them the scientific process that men and women of all ages throughout the world have been following for centuries.

You need to provide young children with the time, opportunities, and materials to be able to experiment on their own, at their own pace, and at their own developmental skill level. Many of the materials for these science experiments are, literally, already at their fingertips through their five senses, natural elements in their surroundings, or common household materials.

Through the following books and ideas, we hope to capitalize on the natural curiosity of children. Remember to share this excitement and quest for answers with your children. Find out (question) what they already know, what misconceptions they have formulated in their efforts to make sense of their world, and what they would like to learn about the topic. Make predictions (hypothesize) about what might happen as you set up before actually trying (experiment) to find an answer. Watch what happens carefully (observe) as the experiment unfolds. Discuss and write down with words or pictures (record) your findings after you experiment. Evaluate the results and extrapolate new knowledge that has been gained (conclude). In this way, the child learns to mimic the work of a scientist.

SCIENCE SKILLS FOR YOUNG CHILDREN TO LEARN

The science extension activities demonstrate many science skills. The following are descriptions of those skills that are highlighted in our various activities.

Cause and Effect—This means if one thing happens, it will result in a certain outcome, which can be measured by a positive or negative correlation between the two. For instance, a possible hypothesis for cause and effect might be, "If we do not water a plant, it will die." If this is always true, there is a positive correlation of one and a perfect example of cause and effect. Conversely, the statement "If we repeatedly eat chocolate ice cream but also exercise regularly, we will not gain weight" might not have such a positive correlation for some!

Communicating and Recording—These skills are necessary to advance knowledge in the sciences around the world. For young children to fully grasp new concepts, they must articulate their thoughts and verbalize descriptive terms. By providing a written account of their results, whether it be in pictures, numbers, or words (dictated if necessary), children can look back and refer to their findings again and again.

Comparing, Contrasting, and Matching—Children learn to distinguish and sort similarities from differences. Comparing involves finding those things that are alike and those that are different between two or more objects. Contrasting focuses on just their differences, and matching looks at similarities. Use of containers, a chart, or a Venn diagram of two overlapping hula hoops (*see Each Living Thing* below) is helpful for organizing the resulting sort.

Designing, Constructing, and Problem Solving—Figure out how to construct something either through planning or simply by trial and error. Young children need to use actual objects that they can manipulate, while older children may plan on paper.

Devising and Planning Investigations—Children preplan or decide the optimal ways to conduct inquiries. In these cases, the old axiom of "two heads are better than one" often holds true; through group discussions, or simply by pair sharing, children may be introduced to novel ideas for carrying out their studies while also practicing social skills in the process.

Estimating—This "educated" guessing, which improves with practice, is not the actual answer, but it should be somewhat near the correct response, as children's experiences allow. Repeating the process many times helps young children estimate more accurately.

Experimenting or Testing—Children check what really happens when they try their activity. Is their hypothesis true, or did their theory work? Scientists do each experiment many times to confirm their results, and they use controls and variables to verify the cause of what is happening. Instruction in maintaining a control (where nothing is changed) and a variable (where one element is changed) may be helpful.

Exploring—This is a search using various appropriate senses to examine in careful detail facts about an object or event. Children have been naturally doing this, as they are able, since birth.

Finding Patterns and Relationships—Among flora and fauna or rocks and minerals, children sort and compare to see how things fit together or are disparate in our world.

Hypothesizing or Predicting—Children decide upon a possible final outcome or guess a theory to explain something after observing but before performing the actual experiment. By stating a hypothesis, children are motivated not only to think about what they already know, but also to watch the results more carefully because they have some "ownership" of the outcome.

Measuring and Calculating—These help children connect the world of mathematics to science by using the tools of measurement (such as those used for linear, volume, and mass, whether standard English or metric or nonstandard) and the properties of addition, subtraction, multiplication, and division of numbers.

Observation—Children may use more senses than vision to accomplish this close or prolonged scrutiny of an object or event over time. They watch to see what happens or notice how things change or don't change.

Ordering, Sorting, and Classifying—Children put objects into groups based on their attributes of color, shape, size, habitat, diet, species, and so forth. Delineation with a chart or containers is helpful in separating and grouping items.

Reasoning—When employing logical thought, as in hypothesizing, the greater the number of experiences children have had, the less naive their deductions will be. Children figure out why.

Researching—Children consult standard sources of reference books, nonfiction materials, magazines with scientific information, or a reliable Internet source or try things out on their own to find an answer.

Transformation and Reversibility—Change, and the ability or inability to reverse that change, includes irreversible transformations such as the metamorphosis of a caterpillar into a butterfly, the baking of cake or cookie batter, and the growth of an acorn into an oak tree. Some examples of reversibility are the removal of iron filings from a mixture of sand and iron filings by rubbing a magnet through to attract and remove the iron from the sand; or, after dissolving salt in water, causing the water to evaporate so the salt crystals remain. Children may be familiar with this concept if they pick out, for example, the peas from their vegetable soup before consuming it. The peas *were* incorporated with the other vegetables and the broth, but children can undo that by removing them.

HINTS FOR SUCCESS WHEN PERFORMING EXPERIMENTS

We found all of the materials we needed to carry out the experiments already in or around our homes. Although we have tried all of these experiments ourselves, we may not tell you all the answers to each of our questions. Sometimes it is more fun to find out for yourself what happens when you experiment. Therefore, we highly recommend that you do a "dry run" for each experiment before presenting it to a group of children for the first time. Occasionally, despite repeated tries of following the directions during these practice sessions, an experiment may not pan out as planned. By knowing this ahead of time, the adult avoids futile efforts that may be a waste of time for the children involved.

Also, by trying everything first, an adult learns when perseverance is necessary to make an experiment work. One candle-extinguishing activity did not work the first time or the second time, but, finally, it did work! Later, in front of the children, we knew to "try, try again," which became a values lesson for the students as well as a science experiment.

SAFETY FIRST!

Experimenting with science sometimes involves inedible substances, sharp utensils, and heat, among other dangerous elements. Keep these safety reminders in mind as you work with children.

   Use appropriate caution with ingredients that should not be ingested, but *do* allow children to taste any edible ingredients with your permission. Remind them to *always* check with an adult before trying any unknown substances. (A poison control presentation may be helpful here.)

   Be careful with sharp utensils. When you use a knife or scissors yourself, be certain that you lay the utensil in a safe place before, during, and after the experiment. Do not, in the excite-ment of the activity, accidentally put any cutting tool within reach of the children.

   Be considerate of the delicate balance of nature. Do not remove living things from their environment. If you "borrow" insects or other creatures to observe, return them to their same habitat at the end of the observation period.

   Warn children about heat sources and label them as places to avoid. Treat matches in the same manner as sharp utensils and nonedibles, above. You may remind the children that Smokey Bear wants them to "Always Be Careful" and "Never Play with Matches."

Please feel free to extend any of our experiments into other areas as the children ask questions and wonder, "What if . . . ?" It *is* OK not to know all the answers all the time. Have fun using our hands-on science activities to stimulate children's learning and natural inquisitiveness.

SCIENCE EXTENSIONS

Alphabet City
Stephen T. Johnson
(Viking)

Incredible paintings that appear as photographs depict letters of the alphabet found in a city setting. From the end of a reinforced sawhorse for an *A* to the angles of fire escape steps along a building for the *Z*, children will be challenged to discover each letter on a new page. Johnson used hot pressed watercolor paper for the paintings, which were designed with pastels, gouache, watercolors, and charcoal.

EXTENSION: **Outdoor Walk**

MATERIALS

   camera (optional)

PROCEDURE

Take children on a walk outside and see if they can find some man-made or naturally occurring letters in the environment using the scientific skills of observing and exploration. You may photograph these with a camera and display them in the room in alphabetical order. This provides the children with a different way of viewing their world, by noticing just the lines and curves that form letters within a whole object.

RECOMMENDATIONS

If weather does not permit outdoor observing, go on a walk inside. Or do both an indoor and outdoor walk and see in which environment you can find more letters. You may wish to take along a clipboard, marker, and a list of alphabet letters to note which letters have been located and where.

ADDITIONAL EXTENSIONS

Have the children use their bodies to make letters of the alphabet. Which letters can they make by themselves? Which letters require the help of a friend? How many different ways can they find to make one letter? Search other alphabet books to see how illustrators picture their letters of the alphabet.

Apples
Gail Gibbons
(Holiday House)

Gibbons provides an in-depth look at how apples grow, how they are harvested, and how they are used. Diagrams include types of apples, how a bee pollinates a blossom, the parts of an apple, how to plant and care for an apple tree, and recipes for pie and cider. Bordered pictures clearly illustrate the very informative text.

EXTENSION: Seed Estimation

MATERIALS

> various varieties of apples
> knife
> red poster board or paper cut in the shape of an apple
> crayon or colored marker

PROCEDURE

Show the children an uncut apple and ask them to estimate how many seeds the apple contains. On the apple-shaped poster, record the children's guesses. Then, cut the apple in half horizontally so that you can see the star pattern made by the seeds. Count the number of seeds. (*See* Fibonacci numbers under *Math Curse* in chapter 5.) Repeat this experiment with different varieties of apples. Children will use scientific skills of estimation, counting, hypothesizing, observing, reasoning, and problem solving.

RECOMMENDATIONS

Older children may use plastic or metal table knives and cut the apples themselves. We recommend that you cut the apples for younger children and place the knife in a safe place when finished. Children may eat the apples after the experiment.

ADDITIONAL EXTENSIONS

Talk about what the children observed. Did they discover there are five sections in each apple with one or two seeds in each section? Using additional apples, cut them into quarters or other fractions for a math extension. For a music extension, sing Raffi's "Apples and Bananas," from his recording *One Light, One Sun*. Or, finally, use the traditional rhyme, "Away Up High in an Apple Tree," adapted below. Each child may take turns being the apple tree. Place two felt apples on the child's shirt and shake the child gently to release the apples.

> Away up high in an apple tree,
>
> Two red apples smiled at me.
>
> I shook that tree as hard as I could;
>
> Down came the apples and,
>
> Mmmm, were they good!

Astro Bunnies
Christine Loomis; illustrated by Ora Eitan
(Putnam)

After the Astro Bunnies see a star in the night sky, they decide they would like to visit it. They climb aboard a rocket ship and see planets, shooting stars, craters, comets, and the Milky Way; they gather moondust; they meet bunnies from another place in space; and they return home. The rhymed text can be sung to the tune of "Twinkle, Twinkle Little Star." The predominantly dark night-sky pages display mixed-media art, including gouache and computer techniques.

EXTENSION: Constellations

MATERIALS

> black paper
>
> self-stick stars
>
> yellow, gold, or silver tempera paint
>
> paint dish or Styrofoam dish
>
> framed window screen (or screen mesh taped on a cardboard frame)
>
> old toothbrush

PROCEDURE

Have children create a constellation with black paper and self-stick stars. For younger children, you might wish to put a chalk outline of a common constellation (e.g., the Big Dipper) on the paper first and have the children use the star stickers to help make constellations. When finished, children may add a spatter-painted smaller star background as depicted in the book illustrations. Holding an encased screen over their pictures, they may dip their toothbrushes into yellow or gold paint and then rub the toothbrushes across the screen. The paint will splatter across the black paper, giving a starlike effect. Science skills include finding patterns and relationships and comparing and contrasting (different constellations).

RECOMMENDATIONS

Make sure you encase the screen to protect children from cutting their hands on sharp wire edges.

If you use silver self-stick stars you may wish to use the silver paint for a background, while gold or yellow paint would be effective with gold self-stick stars.

ADDITIONAL EXTENSIONS

Have children make "moondust" rocks. Using colored pebbles, have children dip them in glue and then shake them inside a resealable bag containing gold or silver glitter. Let the pebbles dry before taking them home. Older children may use a hammer and nail to poke holes into a canning jar lid (*see* the *Turtle Splash!* extension in chapter 5) in the design of a constellation and then place it over a flashlight to project it onto a wall. Serve star- or moon-shaped cookies.

Bugs! Bugs! Bugs!
Bob Barner
(Chronicle)

Vivid colors enhance the appealing bugs in this nonsensical book of rhyme. Actual bug sizes are displayed, and a Bug-O-Meter chart shows eight different bugs and answers the following questions: "Can It Fly?" "Where Does It Live?" "How Many Legs?" and "Does It Sting?" The author-illustrator works with pen and ink, watercolor, and both cut and torn paper and also adds computer graphics.

EXTENSION: A Bug's World

MATERIALS

> a clear container
>
> screen
>
> food
>
> pencils and paper (optional)

PROCEDURE

In these two combined experiments, children will first observe and then pretend to be a bug, seeing what the rest of the world looks like to a bug. For the first activity, use a clear container (such as a plastic jar) with its lid replaced by a screen with wide openings. Have the children add a small amount of sweet or greasy food to the jar. Place the jar on its side in a secluded outdoor area with a label, "Do Not Disturb—Science Experiment in Progress." Have the children check the container after ten or fifteen minutes to see if any bugs have foraged for food. Children can do the second part of this experiment while they wait to see if they bait any bugs. For the second part, have children lie down on the ground and pretend to be a bug. What does grass look like close-up? How large is a stone? How does a tree look when viewed from the ground? What about a human's appearance? Have them state or record their observations. Then, return to the bug bait. Observe any bugs and record their activity. Science skills include observing, finding relationships, communicating through recording, comparing, experimenting, and exploration.

RECOMMENDATIONS

Talk with the children about what type of food would be best to use for bug bait. If you do not lure any bugs, you may dig for bugs in soil or turn over a rock that is on the ground. Bugs may also be purchased in a pet store.

ADDITIONAL EXTENSIONS

Share the nonfiction book *Bugs Are Insects,* by Anne Rockwell, or *Have You Seen Bugs?* by Joanne Oppenheim. Explain why a spider is not an insect: insects have six legs, three body parts (head, thorax, and abdomen), two antennae, and usually have wings. Spiders have eight legs and two body parts. Also discuss the differences between bugs and beetles (bugs are squishy; beetles have hard shells). Have the children make fingerprint bugs, beetles, or noninsects (e.g., a spider) by placing their fingers on an ink pad and making prints on paper as shown in figure 6.1. Five or six fingerprints make a long caterpillar; one and a half fingerprints with legs could be a spider; two fingerprints with two thumbprints along the edges of a thin three-part body, with a few extra lines for its six legs and two antennae, could become a butterfly. Finally, share a song that explains about the different parts of an insect. "I Am an Insect," which is sung to the tune of "Bingo," can be found on the recording *Tickle Tune Typhoon Singing Science.*

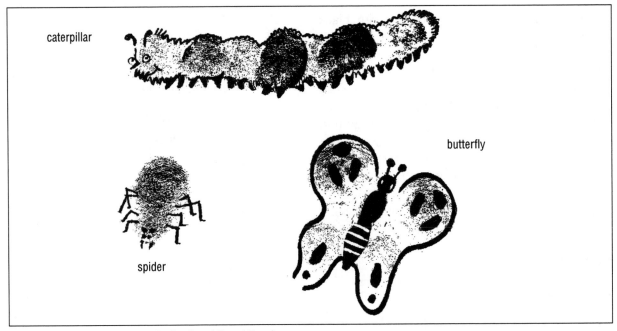

caterpillar

spider

butterfly

FIGURE 6.1 ~ Fingerprint Art for *Bugs! Bugs! Bugs!*

Each Living Thing

Joanne Ryder; illustrated by Ashley Wolff
(Harcourt Brace)

A rhyming text explains why it is important to protect insects and other animals in nature, to respect them, and not disturb them. Children from diverse cultures and different geographic regions are shown practicing good habits to protect nature. Beautiful double-page spreads are rendered in black gesso and gouache.

EXTENSION: **Animals and Their Habitats**

MATERIALS

> animal pictures
>
> picture or drawing of land
>
> picture or drawing of water
>
> picture or drawing of the sky

PROCEDURE

Hold up pictures of animals and ask children where the animals reside. Have the children place the animal pictures on the appropriate drawing of their habitat. Do some animals live or travel in more than one area? Why is it important that an animal remains undisturbed in its own habitat? What are some of the consequences if an animal is removed from its habitat? Some science skills include matching, raising questions, and reasoning.

RECOMMENDATIONS

If you have difficulty finding animal pictures, you can order them from Newbridge: P.O. Box 1270, Littleton, MA 01460; 800-867-0307, or use word cards with animal names written on them. Call out the names of animals and ask the children where those animals reside. Another way you can do this activity is to use three hula hoops or large circles of yarn with labels for the land, water, and sky, and have the children separate the animals by habitat as shown in figure 6.2. They will soon discover that the circles need to overlap for such animals as ducks or frogs, which spend time in more than one area. For another example of a Venn diagram, *see Five Creatures* in chapter 5.

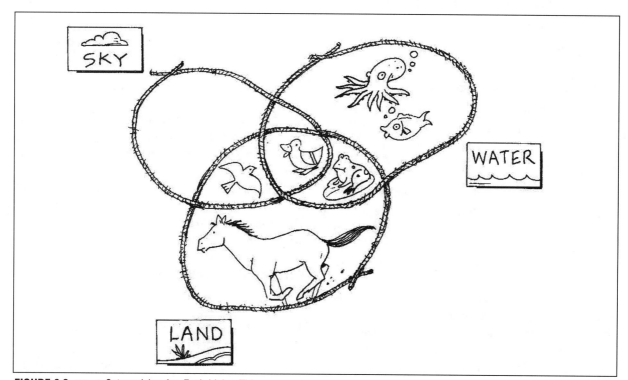

FIGURE 6.2 ~ Categorizing for *Each Living Thing*

ADDITIONAL EXTENSIONS

Share two books by Denise Fleming: *In the Small, Small Pond* and *In the Tall, Tall Grass.* Both books describe animals you would find in those specific locales. Have the children help make up verses sung to the tune "Here We Go 'Round the Mulberry Bush." Examples are "This is the way we swim in a pond . . . when we are a fish," or "This is the way we slink through the grass . . . when we are a snake."

Growing Frogs
Vivian French; illustrated by Alison Bartlett
(Candlewick)

A mother and daughter read a story about frogs and then go to a man-made pond, retrieve some spawn, and grow frogs. Later, they return the frogs to the same pond. Warm- and cool-colored acrylics accompany the whimsical text.

EXTENSION: **Growing Frogs**

MATERIALS

> frog spawn from man-made pond
>
> bucket
>
> pond weed
>
> stones
>
> additional pond water
>
> a fish tank
>
> screen (optional)

PROCEDURE

This book gives very explicit directions on how to grow frogs from spawn, how to gather the spawn, what to feed the tadpoles, and how to provide an environment for the newly developed frogs, so we recommend that you follow these directions carefully. We have enjoyed observing frogs with many groups of children over the years. They are low-maintenance pets but endlessly fascinating in their eating habits and movements. Science skills for this activity include observing a transformation, devising and planning an investigation, designing, and experimenting.

RECOMMENDATIONS

Make sure you follow the very important rules of nature given in the book. Only take frog spawn from a man-made pond, take only a small amount of spawn—preferably five to eight—and return the grown frogs back to the same man-made pond. You may also wish to share the book *From Tadpole to Frog,* by Wendy Pfeffer.

ADDITIONAL EXTENSIONS

Discuss the differences between frogs and toads. Frogs have smooth, shiny, and sometimes greenish skin. Toads have rough, bumpy, and often brown skin that some people refer to as "wart-like." Frogs' noses are longer, while toads' are more blunt. Frogs sleep in the mud or ponds when they hibernate; toads sleep in the ground. Frogs like to eat in the daytime, toads at night. Frogs reside in moist or wet areas such as ponds; toads like the dry earth. Toads are also friendlier to humans. For another extension, play a game of leapfrog. Older students may enjoy the *Frog and Toad* "I Can Read" series by Arnold Lobel.

Hello, Red Fox
Eric Carle
(Simon & Schuster)

Red Fox invites his friends to his birthday party, but his mom becomes confused about what color each animal is. Carle has employed a process whereby readers stare at a certain animal's color and then look at the next page (completely white), where they will then see the complimentary color. The illustrations are his classic cut-paper collages alternated by the blank white pages.

EXTENSION: **Color Illusion**

MATERIALS

> one hard-cooked egg for each pair of children
>
> dark-colored washable (not permanent) markers

PROCEDURE

Using dark-colored markers (red, green, blue, purple, etc.), have pairs of children draw pea-sized dots of color in any pattern all over an egg. Have them spin the egg, and they will see rings of color instead of individual dots because their eyes perceive the colored spots as different colored rings, an optical illusion. Science skills include observing, raising questions, and reversibility.

RECOMMENDATIONS

Have the person who boils the eggs prick the rounded end of the egg with a fine-point needle to help keep the eggshell from cracking during the boiling process. (There is also a commercially made product developed to prick eggs for this purpose.) This process is similar to pricking a potato skin before cooking it to keep the skin intact. Hot air has an escape route and prevents bursting and breaking. When the children have completed their experiments with the hard-cooked eggs, they may peel, wash, and then cut their shared eggs in half and enjoy eating them.

ADDITIONAL EXTENSIONS

Demonstrate the same experiment using an uncooked egg and compare the results. Does it spin as well? Does it spin the same way? Does it spin long enough so that you can see rings? Which is the best position to view the rings on the eggs as they spin: from the top of the egg, or from its side? Does the egg spin as well on both its ends (vertically) as it does on its middle (horizontally)? Children will be using additional science skills of predicting, hypothesizing, raising questions, and testing. Then, share a picture book about eggs; two good titles are David Kirk's *Humpty Dumpty* or Kevin O'Malley's *Humpty Dumpty Egg-Splodes*.

How Do Dinosaurs Say Good Night?
Jane Yolen; illustrated by Mark Teague
(Blue Sky)

The recurring question, "How does a dinosaur say good night?" is answered by a series of responses describing undesirable behaviors, with a final description of ideal conduct. Different types of dinosaurs are depicted on each page, and observant children will see the dinosaur name hidden somewhere within the picture. With a rhyming text, this makes a perfect bedtime story, but it will also be enjoyed by young dinosaur lovers any time of the day. Teague's double-page spreads depicting large, colorful dinosaurs with playful expressions are sure to be a hit.

EXTENSION: Clay Dinosaur Models

MATERIALS

> modeling dough (*see* chapter 2 under *The Party* for the recipe), clay, or Crayola Model Magic

PROCEDURE

Let each child choose a mound of modeling dough or clay to form into a model dinosaur. Children may be interested in looking at pictures or plastic models of dinosaurs to reproduce specific features. Some children will pull out various features from the mound of dough itself, while others will break off clumps to roll into legs, necks, heads, and tails to attach to the body. Some children may want to make dinosaur eggs, perhaps with a part of the baby emerging. For other dinosaur activities, see Mick Manning and Brita Granstrom's *Dinomania*. Science skills include researching, designing, constructing, and problem solving.

RECOMMENDATIONS

Plastic-coated place mats make excellent bases on which to roll out and design modeling dough or clay. They protect the table or desk surface and are sturdy enough to move to a drying location without disturbing the child's creation. They are easily stored, and often may be obtained for free as recyclables.

ADDITIONAL EXTENSIONS

Make a painted papier-mâché diorama in which to place the finished modeling-dough creatures. Provide a large, flat, cardboard base for each group of children as shown in figure 6.3. Before starting, the children should decide where to place hills, volcanoes, land, water, and trees. Use resource books to be accurate for a desired era or period, if appropriate. For hills and volcanoes, crumple wads of newspaper and temporarily tape them in place. For trees, use various heights of paper towel rolls as the trunks, and balance or tape them in place as desired. Have the children tear long strips of newspaper an inch or two wide to dip into a flour-and-water mixture the consistency of heavy cream and use their first two fingers as a V to strip off any excess goop. This will be messy, so have plenty of extra newspaper or an old picnic cloth as a floor covering. Have the children lay the strips of wet newspaper over the crumpled wads of newspaper, extending out to the cardboard base on each side. This will provide the top surface of the hills and volcanoes, as well as

anchor the landform to the cardboard base. Continue to cover the surface of the hill or volcano until there is a smooth and finished look over the entire area. Volcanoes have a hole pushed into the center as a crater. Meanwhile, add additional strips of the wet newspaper around the bases of each of the trees, to anchor them in place. Allow the applied strips to dry thoroughly. For a sturdier finished product, the children may add a second and even a third layer of newspaper strips, dipped in flour and water. In this case, use colored newspaper, such as the Sunday comics (but do *not* use glossy inserts, which won't absorb the flour-and-water mixture), to distinguish where the children need to add the strips for the second layer. Allow each layer to dry thoroughly before painting the top layer. Traditionally, the water area is painted blue or covered with aluminum foil, while the hills and volcanoes may be green, brown, yellow, gray,

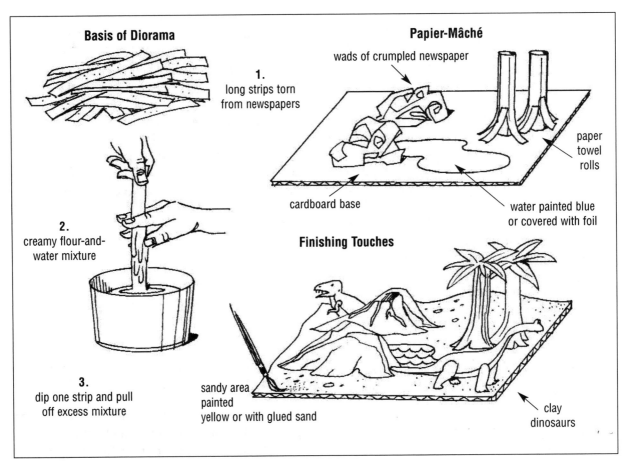

Basis of Diorama

1. long strips torn from newspapers

Papier-Mâché

wads of crumpled newspaper

paper towel rolls

cardboard base

water painted blue or covered with foil

2. creamy flour-and-water mixture

Finishing Touches

3. dip one strip and pull off excess mixture

sandy area painted yellow or with glued sand

clay dinosaurs

FIGURE 6.3 ~ Dinosaur Diorama for *How Do Dinosaurs Say Good Night?*

black, or red. Sand glued along the water's edge or dirt or small stones glued on make some areas seem more authentic. Have the children add leaves to the trees with crepe or construction paper attached to the tops of the tubes. Crepe paper also works well for lava from a volcano. Place dinosaurs as desired around the diorama, in or near the water or vegetation. Dinosaur eggs may be placed in a nesting area. Discuss the finished product with the children. Display this for a few weeks where others may also enjoy the results.

I Will Never Not Ever Eat a Tomato
Lauren Child
(Candlewick)

Charlie needs to feed his younger sister Lola her dinner, but she is a very finicky eater with a long list of foods that she will not eat. Charlie subtly tricks her into believing the vegetables and fish sticks are other foods from under the sea or outer space. Soon Lola is eating all kinds of vegetables, including moonsquirters (tomatoes). The illustrations are mixed media with photographs of real foods in the collage.

EXTENSION: **Identification of Fruits and Vegetables by Smell and Taste**

MATERIALS

> various types of fruits and vegetables cut in small pieces
>
> a blindfold or recycled necktie
>
> plates or cups

PROCEDURE

Cut up each fruit and vegetable, placing the small pieces of each on an individual plate or cup. Blindfold the children, one at a time, and have them guess what the food is on each plate by smelling and tasting a piece. Can they identify the fruit or vegetable? Which sense was more important in the identification? Did students also need to rely on the texture of the food? (This would involve using the sense of touch.) Science skills include testing, comparing, researching smells and tastes, and predicting.

RECOMMENDATIONS

Add some unusual fruits or vegetables so children will be exposed to new produce. Have them taste the product first (without the blindfold). Kiwi, persimmon, star fruit, kumquat, papaya, mango, rutabaga, plum, radish, pea pods, turnips, cabbage, and eggplant are examples. For younger children, use only one or two unusual items of produce so that the experiment is not too difficult, and mention what the choices are ahead of time.

ADDITIONAL EXTENSIONS

Have children give applicable outer space or undersea names to other fruits and vegetables (including some of the more unusual ones) based on their characteristics. Then, talk about what types of food astronauts eat while traveling in outer space. For web sites that supply such information, check <http://spacelink.nasa.gov/Instructional.Materials/NASA.Educational.Products/Space.Food.and.Nutrition> for an educator's guide with activities in science and math or <http://www.nasaexplores.com/lessons/01-022/index.html> for an excellent guide on "Just What Do Astronauts Eat during Space Flights?" and "No Pizza in Space," including lesson plans for grades K through four, five through eight, and nine through twelve. Check a local sporting goods store for some space-type freeze-dried foods or purchase online at <http://www.mountainhouse.com/index. html>.

Kiss the Cow!
Phyllis Root; illustrated by Will Hillenbrand
(Candlewick)

Mama May sings a song to Luella the cow every day to get her pail of milk to feed her many children, and then she kisses Luella right on the end of her nose. Annalisa ignores her mother's pleas not to milk the magic cow and sneaks off to get a pail of milk, but then she refuses to kiss the cow. Luella becomes despondent and will give no milk for the hungry family until Annalisa gives in and finally kisses the cow! The whimsical illustrations are mixed media on vellum.

EXTENSION: **Using Milk to Make Chocolate Ice Cream**

MATERIALS

> 1 tablespoon of cocoa
> 1 tablespoon of sugar
> 1 1/2 tablespoons of very warm water
> 1/2 cup 2% milk
> 1/2 teaspoon of vanilla
> 15 to 18 ice cubes
> 8 tablespoons of coarse salt or rock salt
> measuring cups and spoons
> spoons for tasting
> 2 gallon-sized resealable bags
> 1 quart-sized resealable bag
> paper towels

PROCEDURE

Have the children measure and gently shake cocoa, sugar, and warm water together in the quart-sized resealable bag until the cocoa and sugar dissolve. Then, help them add milk and vanilla to this mixture and seal the bag. Place the quart-sized bag inside one of the gallon-sized bags. Add ice cubes and salt to the gallon-sized bag and seal it tightly. Place this bag into another gallon-sized bag to make it a double thickness in case the first bag leaks. Have children take turns shaking the bagged mixture for eight minutes or until the ice cream thickens. They will need to hold the bags with a paper towel or padding because of the coldness. When the ice cream is frozen, unseal the bags and let the children enjoy tasting their homemade ice cream! This will serve approximately twenty children, a teaspoonful for each child. Science skills include measuring, observing a transformation, and cause and effect.

RECOMMENDATIONS

Make the same recipe above minus the cocoa and hot water to supply vanilla ice cream for any children who are allergic to chocolate. Older children may each make their own individual bags of ice cream. We allow the younger children to share, because they will tire of shaking before the mixture freezes. Afterward, serve store-bought ice cream and have children compare the texture, flavor, consistency, and appearance.

ADDITIONAL EXTENSIONS

You can also make another dairy product from whipping cream. Have children help put two marbles into an empty baby food jar or small, clear peanut butter container and fill the jar three-fourths full of whipping cream. Twist the lid on tightly. Put packaging tape around the lid to secure it. Pass the jar around so each child can help shake it until it turns into butter. The longer you shake it, the more solid the butter becomes. Pour off the remaining buttermilk, which may be tasted or used in a recipe that calls for it. Serve the butter to children on crackers or slices of bread cut into circles and folded into the shape of a kiss.

Miss Spider's Tea Party
David Kirk
(Scholastic)

Miss Spider is lonely and wants some company so she decides to host a tea party. However, when she tries to invite different insects, they all refuse, thinking that she will eat them! Finally, one wet moth attends, and the others decide to take a chance. In addition to the story, this is a counting book with numerals from one to ten. The dramatic full-page spreads are rendered in oil paint.

EXTENSION: **Spider Webs**

MATERIALS

> duct tape, masking tape, or double-sided tape

PROCEDURE

The purpose of this experiment is to understand why spiders do not get caught in their own webs.

The answer is that not all of the web threads are sticky. First, spiders spin the vertical threads, which are not sticky, and then they spin the horizontal threads, which are sticky. Spiders know they can only walk on their vertical threads, while other insects get caught on the horizontal ones. To show children how a spider web works to catch insects, with one child playing the spider and the other the insects, place three-foot strips of duct tape, sticky side down, in a wheel formation on the floor, with the spokes of tape radiating out from the center as shown in figure 6.4. Between the spokes place pieces of duct tape sticky side up, connecting one spoke to the next. Fasten the ends of each piece of sticky tape to the spokes by turning the cut edges down and flattening them against the spokes. Continue doing this, connecting sticky tape between all the spokes. Now, have the children see what it is like to tread on a spider's web. One child, as the spider, may sit in the center. The other children attempt being a spider by walking on the web to the center and back to the edge. Those who become stuck identify themselves as insects. Those who traverse the web without getting stuck on the tape are the fellow spiders. Science skills include designing, experimenting, problem solving, and reasoning.

RECOMMENDATIONS

Use silver duct tape to give the effect of spider web threads. Older children can help place the tape on the floor in the formation of an observed web. It is not necessary to form an entire circular web, because the technique becomes clear with only a portion of it designed.

ADDITIONAL EXTENSIONS

Share Eric Carle's picture book *The Very Busy Spider* or Iza Trapani's *Itsy Bitsy Spider*. Follow the latter title by singing the traditional song, or sing Raffi's song "Spider on the Floor," available on his recording *Singable Songs for the Very Young*. Hold a "Miss Spider Tea Party." Drink green Kool-Aid and serve tiny cupcakes with gummy spiders on top. (Or use plastic spiders, but make sure kids remove them before eating!)

FIGURE 6.4 ~ Spider Web for *Miss Spider's Tea Party*

My Fire Engine
Michael Rex
(Henry Holt)

A young boy imagines what it would be like to be a real fireman and fight fires, including rescuing the family's pet snake. The author-illustrator used pencil on paper and hand separated the colors to make the brightly hued illustrations.

EXTENSION: **Extinguish the Candle**

MATERIALS

tall candle

matches

quart jar

vinegar

1 tablespoon of baking soda

water

small fire extinguisher or bucket of water

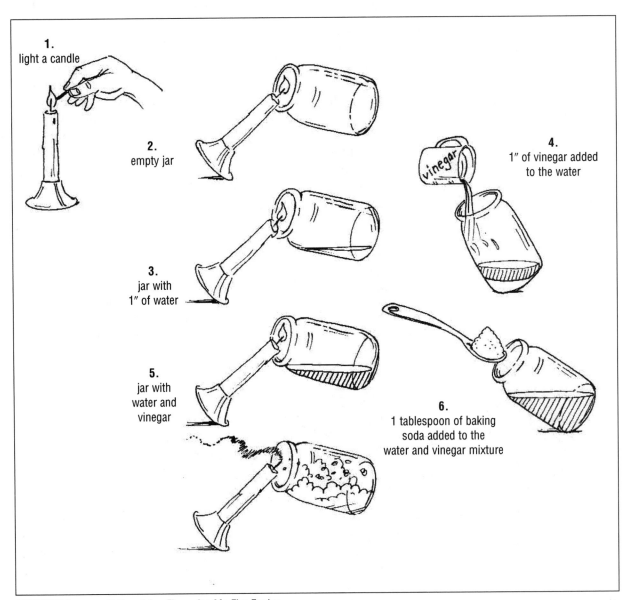

1. light a candle

2. empty jar

3. jar with 1" of water

4. 1" of vinegar added to the water

5. jar with water and vinegar

6. 1 tablespoon of baking soda added to the water and vinegar mixture

FIGURE 6.5 ~ Extinguish a Flame for *My Fire Engine*

PROCEDURE

Have a small fire extinguisher or bucket of water on hand as you do this experiment. Caution children to stay safely seated a few feet away. Discuss each of the following actions with children before you demonstrate. Challenge the children to predict what will happen each time. Follow the procedure shown in figure 6.5. Light a candle and put it into a tilted jar for a few seconds. Children will note that the candle does not extinguish itself. Next, pour about an inch of water into the jar. Again, put the tip of the candle inside the tilted jar for a few seconds. They will see that the candle stays lit. Try the same thing after adding an inch of vinegar to the water. Children will see that it continues to burn. Ask children what they predict will happen if you put baking soda into the jar with the water and vinegar. With children watching, add a tablespoon of baking soda. As they see the carbon dioxide bubbles forming, put the candle into the container a fourth time. The carbon dioxide bubbles should extinguish the flame. Science skills include predicting, observing, problem solving, communicating, experimenting, and raising questions.

RECOMMENDATIONS

Be very careful with fire around the children. You may want to have the baking soda measured into a small container for the children to add, so that you can use your hands for the lit candle and the jar. The candle should have either a holder or a glob of clay stuck on the bottom so it will stand by itself.

ADDITIONAL EXTENSIONS

Ask the children if they know that fire needs three things to burn: heat, oxygen, and fuel. Tie this into a lesson on "Stop, Drop, and Roll." By rolling, they smother the flames, just as the carbon dioxide did. Have them practice this procedure by dropping to the floor and rolling as they cover their faces with their hands. Have a local firefighter dressed in firefighter gear visit the library or classroom so children can see the protective clothing that firefighters wear to keep them from burning. Perhaps the children can try on the coat, boots, gloves, or helmet. Learn how firefighters extinguish fires by using water to cool the flames, chemicals to prevent oxygen from reaching the flames, and by removing the fuel supply. Two other excellent picture books to share are *Firefighters A to Z* by Chris L. Demarest and *Stop, Drop, and Roll* by Margery Cuyler.

Soap! Soap! Don't Forget the Soap!
Tom Birdseye; illustrated by Andrew Glass
(Holiday House)

Plug is a forgetful boy who cannot remember anything unless he keeps repeating it out loud. When his mom sends him to the general store to purchase soap, he keeps repeating "Soap! Soap! Don't forget the soap!" but, unfortunately, others he meets on the way misunderstand and thus distract him, causing him to repeat alternate phrases. Fortunately, a chance encounter gets him back to his soap refrain so he is finally able to purchase what his mother wants. This is a cumulative tale from Appalachia. Reds, yellows, and browns predominate in the sketchy line-filled drawings.

EXTENSION: **Soap Bubble Shapes**

MATERIALS

> Dawn or Joy dishwashing liquid
>
> glycerin
>
> wire clothes hangers
>
> safety scissors
>
> canning jar rings
>
> slotted spoons
>
> large tray or child-sized wading pool

PROCEDURE

Add equal amounts of water and dishwashing liquid to a large tray or child-sized wading pool. Add a tablespoon or two of glycerin for a large quantity of soap solution to make the bubbles stronger. Bend wire clothes hangers in various shapes, and have children dip the shapes completely into the soap solution. Have them observe the colors swirling on the soap film before blowing the bubble and then see the colors that appear when light reflects from the bubble. They can also pull the clothes-hanger wands through the air quickly instead of blowing bubbles—the bubbles will form on their own. Have the children experiment with other objects—scissor handles, canning jar rings, slotted spoons—and see what shapes are formed. You may also have children dip their hands in the soap solution, holding their forefinger to their thumb, to blow small bubbles. Science skills include exploration, experimenting, finding patterns and relationships, observing, and comparing and contrasting.

RECOMMENDATIONS

Be sure to use either of the brand names for the liquid dishwashing products to make the best bubbles. Glycerin, which stabilizes the bubbles, can be purchased at a drugstore or discount department store. Wands can be made with coat hangers, chenille stems, or straws (bundle straws together with a rubber band to make many tiny bubbles). Wands may also be purchased from an early childhood education materials catalog, such as Discount School Supply, 800-627-2829 or <http://www.DiscountSchoolSupply.com>. This experiment should be held outdoors if possible, away from traffic, on a calm, humid day.

ADDITIONAL EXTENSIONS

Sing the song "I'm Forever Blowing Bubbles" (written in the early 1900s by Jaan Kenbrovin, a pseudonym originated by musicians James Kendis, James Brockman, and Nat Vincent). For an additional art activity, divide the soap solution into four containers and add a few drops of food coloring or one tablespoon of tempera paint in red, yellow, green, and blue, respectively, to each container to make four different colors of bubbles. These are the predominant colors used in the illustrations. Have children blow their bubbles onto white paper and observe the colored splats. For more bubble exploration, check out Kimberly Brubaker Bradley's *Pop! A Book about Bubbles,* in the Let's-Read-and-Find-Out Science series.

Sody Sallyratus
Teri Sloat; illustrated by Andrew Glass
(Dutton)

This classic Appalachian tale involves a squirrel, hungry for some baking soda biscuits, that lives with a family who is out of baking soda. The old woman of the house sends first the boy, then the girl, and finally the old man, one by one, down to the corner grocery store to buy some "sody sallyratus," an old term for baking soda. None of them return, however, so she goes herself. When she does not return, the squirrel investigates and finds a bear has eaten them all. He tricks the bear into following him up a tree. The bear falls from the tree and out pop all the family members from the bear's stomach. They head home to make the baking soda biscuits, with the squirrel getting the biggest share. The art is reproduced on biscuit colored paper and is evocative of an Appalachian setting. The text and some pictures are encased in frames of saplings that are lashed together.

EXTENSION: Baking Powder Bubbles

MATERIALS

> pint jar
>
> 1/2 cup warm water
>
> 1 teaspoon of double-acting baking powder

PROCEDURE

Fill the jar with the warm water and add the baking powder. Ask children what they see. Bubbles of carbon dioxide should form. Next heat the jar for thirty seconds in a microwave oven. Ask the children what is happening now. Bubbles should again appear and begin to foam up the sides of the jar. This demonstrates the double-acting process of the baking powder. It bubbles when it is first added to a liquid mixture in a recipe and then later causes the batter to rise further when heated. Science skills include observing, predicting, cause and effect, testing, and transformation.

RECOMMENDATIONS

At one time, biscuits were made with baking soda (sodium bicarbonate). We used baking powder in our experiment because today baking powder (invented in the 1800s) is usually used. Baking powder includes baking soda and cream of tartar. A note in the back of the book explains this and gives a recipe for baking soda biscuits. Make sure to use fresh baking powder (check the expiration date) or this experiment will not work as effectively.

ADDITIONAL EXTENSIONS

Make the biscuits according to the recipe in the back of the book and serve them with butter and honey. Another idea is to give children twigs and see if they can lash them together with rubber bands to make frames as depicted in the book.

Tops and Bottoms
Janet Stevens
(Harcourt Brace)

A lazy bear inherited wealth from his father and also bought the land from his neighbor, Hare, who had lost a bet with a tortoise. Because Hare's family is hungry, he devises an ingenious plan to trick bear by growing crops, but only after asking the bear if he wants the tops or bottoms of the plants. Once the bear decides, Hare plants vegetables accordingly, so that he ends up with the edible part of the plants and bear gets the useless roots or inedible tops. Bear finally gets angry and plants his own food. Stevens designed her own paper pulp using carrots, corn, potatoes, beans, radishes, tomatoes, and even a pair of gardening pants and a shirt as ingredients in creating her paper. The illustrations were subsequently rendered in watercolor, colored pencil, and gesso. Another unusual fact about this book is that it reads from top to bottom vertically, rather than from left to right.

EXTENSION: Carrot Tops and Bottoms

MATERIALS

> fresh carrots with green tops attached
> knife
> saucer
> water

PROCEDURE

Show the children carrots with the greens attached as depicted in the book. Talk about how the bottom of the carrot is the edible part, while the green tops that grow above the ground are not used. Next break off the green tops of the carrot. Cut off one-half inch from the top of the carrot and place it cut side down in a saucer. Add water so that it covers the bottom half of the carrot. Put the saucer in a sunny location and watch the carrot carefully, adding more water as needed, especially around the fourth day. By the fifth day, carrot greens should begin to reappear. Within a week, they will spike up to an inch tall and will need additional water to continue growing by extending tiny white root hairs into the water. Serving carrot cookies or carrot cake would be an appropriate snack after sharing this story and preparing the carrot top for growth. Science skills include observing, experimenting, measuring, if desired, and transformations.

RECOMMENDATIONS

In a library setting, you may wish to grow the carrot top ahead of time and then give each family a piece of carrot top to take home to try on their own. Buy bunches of carrots with greens attached based on the number of children or families involved in your program. They will stay fresh for a week in a refrigerator.

ADDITIONAL EXTENSIONS

Just like the bear in the story, children can experience not knowing what is planted and how it will grow by giving them mystery seeds. Purchase a variety of vegetable seeds and place them in numbered envelopes to give to each child. Beforehand, record the type of seeds you put in each particular envelope. Children can take them home, plant them, watch them grow, and guess what their mystery plant is. Would they choose tops or bottoms when consuming the resulting vegetable? Another good book to share that describes planting mystery seeds is *The Surprise Garden*, by Zoe Hall.

Tough Cookie
David Wisniewski
(Lothrop, Lee & Shepard)

Tough Cookie, a police detective, lives at the bottom of the cookie jar beneath the lid, processing center, Crocker Observatory, and the Pillsbury Expressway. An evil enemy, Fingers, has snatched his detective friend, Chips. It is *his* job to stop Fingers, but his girlfriend, Pecan Sandy, and the crumbs on the bottom of the jar help, too. The author-illustrator cut intricate designs in watercolor papers and had them photographed to complete the graphics.

EXTENSION: **Play Detective Using Invisible Ink**

MATERIALS

orange juice	saucers
cotton swabs	purple grape juice
white paper	paint brushes

PROCEDURE

Give each child a piece of paper and a cotton swab. Place saucers containing orange juice near the children. Have them draw on the paper using the swabs as brushes and the juice as paint. The orange juice will dry and become nearly invisible. Now, have them spread a wash of grape juice across the "secret message." Voila! The picture reappears. Science skills include devising an investigation, recording, observing, transformation, and cause and effect.

RECOMMENDATIONS

Children may render their secret message first, before the story is presented, so the orange juice has a chance to dry. You may also use lemon juice or watered-down vinegar, but if you use orange juice followed by grape juice, you can serve orange juice, grape juice, and cookies after sharing the story and investigating the science extension. (Orange juice also works better than either of the other two for us.) Some science books recommend heating the message paper with a burning lightbulb or an iron, but this method offers "instant" results, and children can do it by themselves, safely. You might also experiment with a baking soda wash in place of the grape juice.

ADDITIONAL EXTENSIONS

Another clue that detectives often check for is fingerprints. Children could record their own fingerprints by placing each finger on an ink pad and then rolling it across a paper, as the police do. For a wealth of ideas on making animals or other creatures with fingerprints, check *Ed Emberley's Fingerprint Drawing Book*. (See *Bugs! Bugs! Bugs!* in this chapter for suggestions of how to embellish fingerprints to form a spider or an insect.)

Trashy Town
Andrea Zimmerman and David Clemesha;
illustrated by Dan Yaccarino
(HarperCollins)

Mr. Gilly travels around town picking up trash at the school, park, pizza parlor, doctor's office, and all the houses. Children can join in the refrain to "dump it in, smash it down, drive around the Trashy Town." Each time, the question is asked, "Is the trash truck full yet?" Children can respond yes or no. Finally, he has cleaned up the whole town, and there is only one thing left to clean—himself! The art is reminiscent of the illustrations from picture books of the fifties. Objects are solid blocks of bright colors with minimal details.

EXTENSION: **Litter Bags**

MATERIALS

- large paper grocery bags
- homemade vegetable dyes or colored markers, crayons, and other decorative supplies
- recyclable items

PROCEDURE

Provide each child with a recycled paper grocery bag to decorate and take home to use as a litterbag. The colors for the decorations could come from homemade vegetable dyes made by boiling onion skins for yellow, black walnuts for deep brown, sumac berries for pale red, red beets for dark red, purple cabbage for purplish violet, grass or spinach for green, and pumpkin for dark orange. For directions on making colors from nature, check out the excellent book *Berry Smudges and Leaf Prints,* by Ellen B. Senisi. Or children can use colored markers, crayons, or glue on yarn or rickrack to decorate their bags. Have them decide where they will use their litterbags and discuss what can be recycled or reused rather than being placed in the trash. Then, have children sort recyclable items in categories for recycling. Science skills include problem solving; reasoning; and ordering, sorting, and classifying.

RECOMMENDATIONS

To make homemade vegetable dyes to color the bags, put the plant ingredient into a cooking pan and cover with boiling water. Allow it to steep until the desired color is reached. For the recycling, decorate boxes instead of bags, and attach a sample can, paper, or plastic container and a recycling symbol on each box so it is readily identifiable. Check what numbers of plastics (e.g., 1, 2) are recycled in your area and determine if materials need to be separated by type or can be recycled all together.

ADDITIONAL EXTENSIONS

In a school setting, ask children to pack a snack or lunch for the day you plan to read this story. After eating, divide what is left into the appropriate piles of cans, bottles, plastics, or food scraps. Food scraps that contain no milk, meat, or grease products may be composted. Collect and weigh the trash that is left afterward. Record this amount. Weigh and record the amounts that will be recycled and composted. Record this amount. Now total the two figures. Use a calculator to find the percentage that can be eliminated from taking a trip to the dump or landfill. (Divide the total amount of recyclables and compost by the entire amount of *all* the leftovers added together.) Can the children plan a packed snack or meal that would contain no trash? Discuss why adding trash to the landfill is harmful for our earth.

Veggie Soup
Dorothy Donohue
(Winslow)

Rabbit decides to create her own recipe for vegetable soup instead of using Great Nana's recipe so she can have a "veggie" soup party. But all her friends bring ingredients that are not vegetables and that they think should be in the dish. After a taste test, Rabbit decides she is missing something and adds spices and her friends' gifts. When they eat the soup, they declare it to be horrible and decide to try again, this time by following Great Nana's recipe, which is included.

EXTENSION: Growing Spices

MATERIALS

> planting cups (such as empty yogurt
> > containers or clear plastic cups)
>
> potting soil
>
> spice seeds
>
> water
>
> trowel or scoop
>
> tray

PROCEDURE

Using a pen or pencil, poke a hole in the bottom of each cup to form a drainage hole. Have each child fill the cup with soil and then water it thoroughly. Allow any excess water to drain away. Provide spice seeds that might be found in a spice cabinet, for example, mustard, celery, or dill. Children can choose which spice seeds they wish to use and sprinkle them onto the damp soil. Cover the seeds with a very thin layer of dry soil, and place the cups on a tray. Watch the spices grow, adding more water as necessary and placing the cups in sunlight once they have sprouted. Discuss the growing process with children. Which seedlings appeared first? Which ones grew tallest or thickest or did not grow at all? If you wish, tie in a lesson on phototropism, or how growing plants turn toward sunlight. Determine how to use the resulting plants. Perhaps children will choose to chop the spices into a salad or use them as a garnish for soup, stew, or a dip. Science skills include cause and effect, observing, communicating, and transformation.

RECOMMENDATIONS

If storing the plants is a problem or time is a factor, the cups may be sent home with the children with a note of explanation for parents. Give care instructions as well as any suggestions on how to use the resulting spices.

ADDITIONAL EXTENSIONS

Make a batch of "Friendship Vegetable Soup." Have each child bring a different vegetable to add to the soup. These may be either precooked or raw. Have the children cut the vegetables with plastic or table knives and add the pieces to a broth or soup base, along with any spices. Heat the ingredients until they are cooked and ready to eat, and then serve the children the soup. Three other excellent books to share are *Growing Vegetable Soup*, by Lois Ehlert; the classic tale *Stone Soup*, by Marcia Brown; and *Fox Tale Soup*, by Tony Bonning.

Waiting for Wings
Lois Ehlert
(Harcourt Brace)

Full pages interspersed with partial pages visually and textually describe the metamorphosis of caterpillars into butterflies. End pages clearly depict different types of caterpillars, chrysalides (the pupae stage), butterflies, and their various parts and identify the flowers on which they feast. There is also a detailed description on how to grow a butterfly garden. Ehlert's outstanding illustrations using bold-colored graphics are a visual delight.

EXTENSION: **Feeding Butterflies in the Wild**

MATERIALS

> new, brightly colored plastic pot scrubbers
> sugar-water mixture
> lids the size of the scrubbers
> paper and pencil

PROCEDURE

Make a sugar-water solution using roughly equal amounts of sugar and water. Give each child a scrubber to place on a lid, and pour sugar water over the scrubber. Tell the children to put their lids outside, near some flowers, if possible. Butterflies will be attracted to the bright color of the scrubber and will feed on the sugar water through their proboscis (a linked pair of hollow, tonguelike tubes that work similar to a pair of straws that uncurl when a butterfly feeds). Butterflies taste with their feet (and hear with their knees!). Discuss the appearance of butterflies, and have children tally those they see. Science skills include raising questions, devising and planning investigations, observing, recording, and classifying.

RECOMMENDATIONS

Do not substitute honey for sugar, as honey can prove harmful for butterflies. In a public library setting, have the children prepare the scrubbers in the library and take them home with them. You can provide instructions for the parents along with observation questions. Have children report back whether their color of scrubber was attractive to the butterflies and also describe the types and numbers of butterflies they saw. For further information on butterflies and, in particular, the monarchs' migration, check these sites: <http://www.thebutterflysite.com>, <http://www.monarchwatch.org>, <http://www.monarchlab.umn.edu>, or <http://www.learner.org/jnorth>.

ADDITIONAL EXTENSIONS

Share a fun story about caterpillars that turn into butterflies called *Clara Caterpillar*, by Pamela

Duncan Edwards. The story is filled with C (/k/) alliteration. For an art idea, have children cut out the shape of a butterfly on black paper. Using cut pieces of tissue paper that they can glue on the black shapes, children can decide if they wish to make a monarch, tiger swallowtail, or painted lady butterfly, as depicted in the back of Ehlert's book, or a creation of their own.

Who Hops?
Katie Davis
(Harcourt Brace)

Questions are posed: Who hops? Flies? Slithers? Swims? Crawls? Each time, three correct answers are given along with one incorrect, silly answer. Children can guess the correct answers and learn about animal movement. Pen-and-ink illustrations with preseparated colors were used on brightly colored art paper.

EXTENSION: **Charting Animal Movements**

MATERIALS

> large chart paper
> animal stickers

PROCEDURE

Divide the chart paper into sections labeled *swim, fly, slither, crawl, hop, walk/run, swing,* and *climb.* Give children different animal stickers, and have them decide on which category of the chart to place their stickers. If the animal moves in more than one way, ask the children if there is another category where the sticker also could be placed. Science skills include matching, sorting, classifying, and reasoning.

RECOMMENDATIONS

Set up the chart to accommodate the particular stickers available, or, depending upon resources, use animal rubber stamps and an ink pad instead. Older children can draw the animal or write its name on the chart. Children may also move like their animals and make their animals' sounds for creative dramatics. If your children enjoy this book, you might also want to share another Katie Davis book, *Who Hoots?*

ADDITIONAL EXTENSIONS

Discuss what else can hop, slither, fly, swim, or crawl. Can a raw egg be made to do any of these? What would happen to it if you tried to make it bounce? The answer is, it would bounce gently without cracking *if* you first soaked it in vinegar for a day. Eggshells, like bones, are hard because of the calcium carbonate in them. The acid in vinegar leaches out the calcium carbonate, so the eggshell feels rubbery and behaves differently when moved; it "hops" when it is dropped from an inch above the surface. Next, predict whether an egg can swim. Drop it in water to see if it "swims" or sinks. Once it is wet, can you make it slither (slide) across a table? What about making the egg "fly"? If you pitch it, encased in a plastic resealable bag, it will fly through the air for an instant before splattering.

Bibliography of Picture Books Used in Science Extensions

Barner, Bob. *Bugs! Bugs! Bugs!* San Francisco: Chronicle, 1999.

Birdseye, Tom. *Soap! Soap! Don't Forget the Soap! An Appalachian Folktale.* Andrew Glass, illus. New York: Holiday House, 1993.

Bonning, Tony. *Fox Tale Soup.* Sally Hobson, illus. New York: Simon & Schuster, 2002.

Bradley, Kimberly Brubaker. *Pop! A Book about Bubbles.* Margaret Miller, illus. New York: HarperCollins, 2001.

Brown, Marcia. *Stone Soup.* New York: Atheneum, 1947.

Carle, Eric. *Hello, Red Fox.* New York: Simon & Schuster, 1998.

_____. *The Very Busy Spider.* New York: Philomel, 1985.

Child, Lauren. *I Will Never Not Ever Eat a Tomato.* Cambridge, Mass.: Candlewick, 2000.

Cuyler, Margery. *Stop, Drop, and Roll.* Arthur Howard, illus. New York: Simon & Schuster, 2001.

Davis, Katie. *Who Hoots?* San Diego: Harcourt Brace, 2000.

_____. *Who Hops?* San Diego: Harcourt Brace, 1998.

Demarest, Chris L. *Firefighters A to Z*. New York: Margaret K. McElderry, 2000.

Donohue, Dorothy. *Veggie Soup*. New York: Winslow, 2000.

Edwards, Pamela Duncan. *Clara Caterpillar*. Henry Cole, illus. New York: HarperCollins, 2001.

Ehlert, Lois. *Growing Vegetable Soup*. San Diego: Harcourt Brace, 1987.

_____. *Waiting for Wings*. San Diego: Harcourt Brace, 2001.

Emberley, Ed. *Ed Emberley's Fingerprint Drawing Book*. Boston: Little, Brown, 2001.

Fleming, Denise. *In the Small, Small Pond*. New York: Henry Holt, 1993.

_____. *In the Tall, Tall Grass*. New York: Henry Holt, 1991.

French, Vivian. *Growing Frogs*. Alison Bartlett, illus. Cambridge, Mass.: Candlewick, 2000.

Gibbons, Gail. *Apples*. New York: Holiday House, 2000.

Hall, Zoe. *The Surprise Garden*. Shari Halpern, illus. New York: Blue Sky, 1998.

Johnson, Stephen T. *Alphabet City*. New York: Viking, 1995.

Kirk, David. *Humpty Dumpty*. New York: Putnam, 2000.

_____. *Miss Spider's Tea Party*. New York: Scholastic, 1994.

Lobel, Arnold. *Frog and Toad*. New York: HarperCollins, 1995.

Loomis, Christine. *Astro Bunnies*. Ora Eitan, illus. New York: Putnam, 2001.

Manning, Mick, and Brita Granstrom. *Dinomania: Things to Do with Dinosaurs*. New York: Holiday House, 2001.

O'Malley, Kevin. *Humpty Dumpty Egg-Splodes*. New York: Walker, 2001.

Oppenheim, Joanne. *Have You Seen Bugs?* Ron Broda, illus. New York: Scholastic, 1998.

Pfeffer, Wendy. *From Tadpole to Frog*. Holly Keller, illus. New York: HarperCollins, 1994.

Rex, Michael. *My Fire Engine*. New York: Henry Holt, 1999.

Rockwell, Anne. *Bugs Are Insects*. Steve Jenkins, illus. New York: HarperCollins, 2001.

Root, Phyllis. *Kiss the Cow!* Will Hillenbrand, illus. Cambridge, Mass.: Candlewick, 2000.

Ryder, Joanne. *Each Living Thing*. Ashley Wolff, illus. San Diego: Harcourt Brace, 2000.

Senisi, Ellen B. *Berry Smudges and Leaf Prints: Finding and Making Colors from Nature*. New York: Dutton, 2001.

Sloat, Teri. *Sody Sallyratus*. Andrew Glass, illus. New York: Dutton, 1997.

Stevens, Janet. *Tops and Bottoms*. San Diego: Harcourt Brace, 1995.

Trapani, Iza. *Itsy Bitsy Spider*. Dallas: Whispering Coyote, 1993.

Wisniewski, David. *Tough Cookie*. New York: Lothrop, Lee & Shepard, 1999.

Yolen, Jane. *How Do Dinosaurs Say Good Night?* Mark Teague, illus. New York: Blue Sky, 2000.

Zimmerman, Andrea, and David Clemesha. *Trashy Town*. Dan Yaccarino, illus. New York: HarperCollins, 1999.

Bibliography of Musical Recordings Used in Science Extensions

Raffi. *One Light, One Sun*. Willowdale, Ont.: Troubador Records, 1985.

_____. *Singable Songs for the Very Young*. Willowdale, Ont.: Troubadour Records, 1985.

Tickle Tune Typhoon Singing Science. Redway, Calif.: Music for Little People, 2000.

Science Resource Books

Bittinger, Gayle. *1-2-3 Science: Science Activities for Working with Young Children*. Torrance, Calif.: Totline, 1993.

Charner, Kathy, ed. *The Giant Encyclopedia of Science Activities for Children 3 to 6: More than 600 Science Activities Created by Teachers for Teachers*. Beltsville, Md.: Gryphon House, 1998.

Claud, Elizabeth, and Gregory De Francis. *Mother Goose Asks "Why?": A Family Activity Guide Introducing Science through Great Children's Literature*. Chester, Vt.: Vermont Center for the Book, 1998.

Hauser, Jill Frankel. *Science Play!: Beginning Discoveries for 2- to 6-year-olds*. Charlotte, Vt.: Williamson, 1998.

Hefner, Christine Roots, and Kathryn Roots Lewis. *Literature-Based Science: Children's Books and Activities to Enrich the K–5 Curriculum*. Phoenix: Oryx, 1995.

Hoffmann, Jane. *Backyard Scientist Series One: 25 Experiments That Kids Can Perform Using Things Found around the House*. Irvine, Calif.: Backyard Scientist, 1987.

Holt, Bess-Gene. *Science with Young Children.* Washington, D.C.: National Assn. for the Education of Young Children, 1989.

Kohl, Mary Ann, and Jean Potter. *Science Arts: Discovering Science through Art Experiences.* Bellingham, Wash.: Bright Ring, 1993.

Moomaw, Sally, and Brenda Hieronymus. *More than Magnets: Exploring the Wonders of Science in Preschool and Kindergarten.* St. Paul, Minn.: Red Leaf, 1997.

Rockwell, Robert E., Elizabeth A. Sherwood, and Robert A. Williams. *Hug a Tree and Other Things to Do Outdoors with Young Children.* Beltsville, Md.: Gryphon House, 1996.

Sheehan, Kathryn, and Mary Waidner. *Earth Child 2000: Earth Science for Young Children: Games, Stories, Activities, and Experiments.* Tulsa, Okla.: Council Oak Books, 1998.

Sherwood, Elizabeth A., Robert A. Williams, Robert E. Rockwell, and Roger A. Williams. *More Mudpies to Magnets: Science for Young Children.* Beltsville, Md.: Gryphon House, 1991.

Sosa, Maria, and Tracy Gath, eds. *Exploring Science in the Library: Resources and Activities for Young People.* Chicago: American Library Assn., 2000.

Straughan, Pat, Linda Garrett, and the Staff of Vermont Center for the Book. *Mother Goose Meets Mother Nature: A Family Activity Guide Introducing Environmental Experiences through Great Children's Literature.* Chester, Vt.: Vermont Center for the Book, 1999.

VanCleave, Janice. *Janice VanCleave's Play and Find Out about Nature: 50 Fun, Easy Experiments and Ideas for Young Children.* New York: John Wiley, 1997.

_____. *Janice VanCleave's Play and Find Out about Science: Easy Experiments for Young Children.* New York: John Wiley, 1996.

Williams, Robert A., Robert E. Rockwell, and Elizabeth A. Sherwood. *Mudpies to Magnets: A Preschool Science Curriculum.* Beltsville, Md.: Gryphon House, 1987.

Author/Illustrator Index

Complete bibliographic citations for works are found
at the end of each chapter.

Title Index

Book titles are in italics. Song and story titles are in quotes. Complete bibliographic citations are found at the end of each chapter.

TITLE INDEX

Sue McCleaf Nespeca heads Kid Lit Plus Consulting, providing speeches, training, and consulting to librarians, teachers, and early childhood educators in the areas of children's literature, early literacy, family literacy, and library services to youth. She provides ongoing youth services consulting for the Northwest Library District in Bowling Green, Ohio, and NOLA Regional Library System in Warren, Ohio. She is an adjunct instructor at Kent State University's School of Library and Information Science and Syracuse University's School of Information Studies. Nespeca, a speaker at more than 200 U.S. workshops and conferences, has written several journal articles and publications, including the book *Library Programming for Families with Young Children* (Neal-Schuman, 1994). Active in the Association for Library Service to Children, she was the first recipient of the Bechtel Fellowship. Nespeca has a master's degree in education in early childhood (Kent State) and a master's degree in library science (University of Pittsburgh).

Joan B. Reeve is a kindergarten teacher in the Gettysburg (Pennsylvania) Area School District and an adjunct faculty member at Harrisburg Area Community College, Gettysburg Campus, teaching early childhood educators. She has promoted differentiated supervision throughout Pennsylvania and has presented workshops on peer coaching, differentiated instruction, and Howard Gardner's multiple intelligences. Reeve is a former coeditor of Gettysburg's Primary Education Research Committee's quarterly newsletter. She has a master's degree in elementary education (Millersville University) and is a reading specialist.